Kaizen for Pharmaceutical, Medical Device & Biotech Industries

Shruti U. Bhat Ph.D (Tech), MBA

Certified Lean Six Sigma Black Belt

First Edition

Business Process Management Systems and Continuous Improvement Executive Guide Series.

Published by Shifting Paradigms Publications, Canada.

Copyright

Disclaimer and FTC Notice

The author and publisher of this book, its digital version, and the accompanying materials have used their best efforts in preparing this book. The information contained in this book has been stated accurately to the best ability of the author and publisher. The information contained in this book is strictly for informational purposes. The author and publisher make no representation, warranties or guarantees implicitly or explicitly with respect to the accuracy, contrary interpretations of the subject matter herein, applicability, fitness or completeness of the contents of this book. The reader will be taking full responsibility for incorporating any ideas or suggestions or methods mentioned in this book. The author and publisher specifically disclaim any liability that is incurred from the use or application of the contents of this book.

ISBN: 978-1-988663-04-3

Dedicated to lovely my sister

Sandhya Bhat

Words can't express enough my love and caring for you...

Table of Contents

About the author

SHRUTI U. BHAT, Ph.D (Tech), MBA, Certified Lean Six Sigma Black Belt

Shruti is an Innovation, Quality-by-Design and Continuous Improvement Expert with a Ph.D in Pharmaceutical Technology, MBA, and Certified Lean Six Sigma Black Belt.

Shruti has turned around failing companies to successful enterprises, helped solve cash-flow problems, improved Operations/ Service levels, and PROFITS. She has successfully driven over 1000 projects on innovation, business process redesign and continuous improvement to satisfied clients worldwide.

Shruti *specializes* in pharmaceuticals, bulk drugs, biotech, engineering, natural products, foods & beverages, medical devices, chemicals, and cosmetics industry verticals. She works with startups, small to mid-size and growing companies in Canada, India, US, Europe and New Zealand to turn strategy and innovation into measurable profits.

Strategic Innovation Management:

Through her customized "Innovation-by-Design" methodology, Shruti provides cutting-edge concepts to create affordable quality products that are "Tough to copy". She helps clients gain first-mover advantage via Design-Thinking based Lean Innovations and drives business growth. She is an authority in 32 different hi-tech manufacturing technologies, including 3D Printing.

Strategic Continuous Improvement:

Shruti's efforts facilitate her clients to reduce operation costs, backorders, variations, defects and product returns.

She designs and drives implementation of eighteen proven business improvement methodologies, such as Kaizen, 5S, Lean Six Sigma, JIT, Poka-Yoke, Hoshin Kanri, CAPA, TQM, Quality-by-design, Agile By strategic use of these techniques, she has significantly reduced production cycle times, COGs (cost of goods) and increased operational efficiency.

She has helped build enterprise teams and coached more than 12,000 employees on topics such as DOE, Continuous improvement, Innovation, and Design thinking.

Shruti is Managing Director at Innoworks Inc. a Canadian Management Consulting company with offices in Vancouver, Calgary, and Toronto. She has authored 5 books, over 90 publications in peer-reviewed international journals and has 25 patents to her credit.

Get in touch with Shruti:

Website: http://www.drshrutibhat.com/

LinkedIn: https://www.linkedin.com/in/drshrutibhat

Twitter: https://twitter.com/shrutiubhat

YouTube: https://www.youtube.com/user/shrutibhat10

Facebook: https://www.facebook.com/Innoworks.Inc

Google+ : https://plus.google.com/+ShrutiBhat

Pinterest: https://www.pinterest.com/drshrutibhat

Innoworks:

Innoworks is a Canadian Management Consulting firm with offices in Vancouver, Calgary, and Toronto.

Business success increasingly hinges on a company's ability to leverage tools, new technology, creative concepts to drive innovation, improve operational efficiency and organizational excellence. Advance your business with Innoworks's Design thinking, Rapid prototyping, Quality-by-Design, Lean innovation, Business transformation and Continuous Improvement Consultation and Training Services.

Innoworks is in the business of helping businesses GROW!

Website: http://www.innoworks.ca/

Video:
https://www.youtube.com/watch?v=g39qYtCG-qI

Preface

A few years ago, I was approached by a CEO of a pharmaceutical contract research company to turnaround his sick unit into a profitable enterprise. This company was dealing with the the development of solid oral dosage forms. To bring about the necessary change, we initiated several Kaizen campaigns companywide, with 360 degrees focus to overhaul all processes and operational systems. We addressed all key areas across the organization including accounts payable/ receivable, material procurement, order processing, suppliers, R&D, scale-up, production, logistics, product dossiers filings, project management, business development, sales & marketing and PR communication processes.

Another key area where Kaizen helped us in a big way was to integrate various client information data sets maintained within different databases on separate systems.

Before Kaizen, everything was disjointed, delayed and everyone was working in silos, leading to waste and lost revenues.

Post Kaizen, there was teamwork and excellent cash-flow!

At the end of nine months, this company's books started showing profits, and from there on, it kept going from 'good to great'. It was an excellent example of a successful transformation.

Unfortunately, this contract research company is not alone in the challenges it has faced. Studies indicate that 88% of business owners in North America struggle to maintain consistent cash-flow.

Key questions to consider are:

- Can your organization benefit from increased workplace productivity?
- Does your team face challenges with reduced R&D budget?
- Does your organization face challenges because of inconsistent or poor cash-flow?
- Do you need to cut corners as you are forced to do more with less?

If you answered 'yes' to any of the above questions, then Kaizen should be your mantra...

Kaizen is an outstanding business tool that helps organizations to achieve new heights!

Kaizen procedures evolved in the automobile industry. Therefore, most of Kaizen literature, publications, books, cite Kaizen implementation in factories such as Toyota, Ford, Mazda and the like.

But work practices within pharmaceutical (medical device and biotech) industry are different from the auto sector.

Regulations, customer demands, competitor landscape, product criteria, facility and environmental needs, employee skills within pharmaceutical (medical devices and biotech) companies are extremely stringent and totally different from the automobile industry. Therefore, 'as is' Kaizen practices from auto sector won't work for pharmaceutical, medical device, and biotech organizations. Kaizen must be customized for these industries, to achieve its full benefits.

So far, there has been no book on Kaizen that is customized to pharmaceutical, medical device, and biotech industries. Having successfully driven more than 250 Kaizen, Lean Six Sigma, and other continuous improvement projects within pharmaceuticals, NHP, medical devices, biotech and healthcare sectors, worldwide for over a decade, I have created real success stories; I felt it will be beneficial to share those techniques and experiences.

This book is a structured approach to designing Kaizen strategies, practices and implementation for pharmaceutical, medical device, and biotech companies.

It is an invaluable resource, an essential tool for all professionals within the pharmaceutical, medical device, biotech organizations i.e. all life sciences and health care companies, interested in employing Kaizen in their workplaces and their personal lives. This book will also facilitate running Kaizen in a manufacturing company and do it at a world-class level.

Get ahead with product innovations, improved laboratory productivity, first to file, increased intellectual property, efficient manufacturing, effective marketing and logistics with KAIZEN.

This book doesn't simply explain Kaizen process features, implementation, and application. The scope of this book is much wide.

This book is meant for small to medium-size pharmaceutical, medical device and biotech research, manufacturing and contract services companies. This book is to-

- Demystify Kaizen and help business leaders in pharmaceutical, medical device, biotech, and all life sciences organizations, irrespective of their size or workplace culture.
- Apply Kaizen to what really matters, that is, 'to achieve business expansion along with increased productivity and profits'.

- Provide practical and useful examples of Kaizen principles that can be executed at various levels: across the organization; within a specific department, business unit or team, as well as for yourself as an individual to further your personal career.

- Improve revenues and create a lasting change using Kaizen principles and techniques.

Kaizen requires very less investment, therefore can be implemented to its full potential even in startups.

Kaizen following startups can have minimal failures!

Some salient features of this book

- It shows pharmaceutical & biotech scientists, design engineers, operators and everyone involved in product development, how to utilize Kaizen- to create innovations, shorten product development times, improve first-to-file rates, conduct successful scale-up and technology transfer to manufacturing sites.

- It shows everyone associated with manufacturing, how to use Kaizen to decrease cycle times, work-in-process & quarantine inventories, the cost of distribution & logistics, improve equipment efficiency, facility capacity utilization and shift output.

- It shows everyone in Human Resources how to use Kaizen to minimize employee turnover, hire and retain talent, and motivate employees to create a difference.

- It shows the company's senior management, stakeholders, finance and other supporting business units, how to use Kaizen to increase ROI (return on investment) while complying with cGMP (*current* Good Manufacturing Practices) and other regulations, address rising competition and counteract fluctuating market economy.

- This book presents useful ideas that one can implement immediately, often at no additional cost.

- It shows how to transform a business from 'good- to- great'. True benefits of Kaizen implementation are realized because, it adds value to your products, increases market share, and drives both top line and bottom line of your business.

Kaizen has mainly been used in Japan and many other SE Asian companies and in Europe. Up until now, it has not gained enough significance in North America, because of which it has not been utilized to its full potential. The root cause is the difference in work culture and corporate governance styles of companies in eastern and western countries; this book totally eliminates this gap.

This book presents Kaizen methodology for direct implementation within a pharmaceutical, medical device, biotech company in east or west. Moreover, this book helps you to customize Kaizen to your company; this book is not a 'vanilla generic'.

In addition, this book is an excellent resource for Kaizen beginners with a lot of real life industry examples, case studies and provides several 'do-it-yourself' exercises, which is of tremendous value, in absence of a Kaizen coach.

Kaizen is not just to 'SAVE' more

Kaizen helps to 'MAKE' more- products, more customers, more revenues ...

Now, let us see what Kaizen is...

Shruti Bhat

Chapter 1: Introduction

In this chapter, we will see ...

- ✓ What is Kaizen?

- ✓ Advantages of Kaizen

- ✓ Limitations of Kaizen

- ✓ Dual Nature of Kaizen

- ✓ Kaizen Philosophies

- ✓ Kaizen Principles

- ✓ When to Introduce Kaizen at your workplace?

Pharmaceutical industry growth unlike few other industries viz. retail, banking etc. is not completely determined by 'value' it brings to its customer. Frustrated customers can easily walk out of a shop and get their product from some other place.

In contrast, pharmaceutical products are unique in the sense, the customer (i.e. patient) doesn't usually have much say in its purchase. Patients usually buy medicines their doctors prescribe or pharmacist dispense (until such time they don't experience any adverse effects). For the medicines where adverse effects are well-known or documented on the product label, patients really have no choice but to take bitter medicine (pun intended).

Also, a patient on a prescription drug may not always have the option to change medication or brand, because of lack of competing brands due to enforced Exclusivity and Patents laws. Even with the advent of generic medicines which offer price benefits, many patients don't prefer to change the pill they have been taking over the years.

Moreover, Kano's model may not strictly apply to Life science industries, because unlike other products, a drug product if not proved safe, efficacious and stable, will just not make it to the market. And this applies to all medicinal products- be it Rx (prescription), OTC (over the counter), medical devices etc.

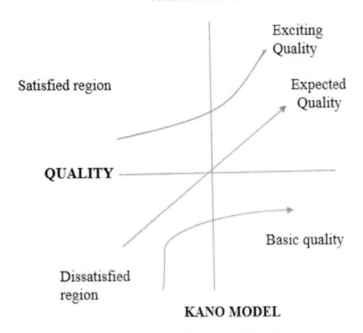

KANO MODEL

Adding to the uniqueness of pharmaceuticals and device industry is that, drug-discovery costs and associated risks keep rising, yet companies have to keep product prices affordable. It is like walking down the stairs of an escalator going up!

Furthermore, pharmaceutical, medical device, and biotech companies are always under federal drug authorities radar for compliance to standards. The very existence of pharma business is based on meeting compliance- be it cGMP, safety, therapeutic efficacy, quality etc.

As federal drug regulations change, companies must upgrade to stay in business.

Hence, there is an indirect continuous improvement happening all the time. This is probably one of the reasons why many life science companies haven't really attempted formal business process improvement methodologies.

However, Kaizen is not simply a business process improvement technique. Kaizen doesn't just focus on cost-cutting or quality improvement. Kaizen is a way of life; of becoming 'better' every day; of becoming better than the best-consistently, and taking your business from being good to great with its products, market share, governance, and *most* importantly, Good to Great with PROFITS!

Let's begin with what is Kaizen?

What is Kaizen?

Kaizen hails from the words, "Renew the heart and make it good." Therefore, an adaptation of Kaizen concept requires changes in the "heart of the business", corporate culture and structure; since Kaizen enables companies to translate the corporate vision in every aspect of its operational practice.

Kaizen

改善

Make Better

The name 'Kaizen' is an adaptation of the Japanese term that stands for continuous improvement. In Kaizen technique, it is believed that employees need to be empowered to enhance various processes of the company. Kaizen utilizes some of the Lean methodology philosophies to plan, implement and evaluate changes in a variety of roles. Kaizen must be integrated into a company's daily operations to achieve maximum benefits.

Kaizen methodology follows PDCA (Plan-Do-Check-Act) as well as W.E Deming's PDSA (Plan-Do-Study-Act), which is a cycle of continuous improvement. Other techniques used in conjunction with PDCA include 5-Whys which is a form of root-cause analysis.

In 5-Whys technique, a user asks "Why" a failure occurred five successive times, wherein each subsequent 'Why' question is based on the answer of the previous one. Thus, Kaizen promotes change in work culture, by allowing and inspiring people to be interested and apply positive alterations to things that matter to them.

Kaizen enhances value and efficiency in processes. It is a procedure that allows companies to reduce waste and costs whilst increasing profitability. It incorporates elements of production such as- flow rate and customer satisfaction. Also, helps companies by analyzing and evaluating resources and processes that are currently in use and checking whether they are still valid or necessary. Processes and resources that are ineffective are removed, replaced or redesigned.

Kaizen has been found to be extremely effective in improving businesses processes that are stagnant, at poor or moderate levels.

A preamble to Kaizen is Value Stream Mapping i.e. a stage in which companies analyze current processes. This step identifies the crucial processes that bring value to the business and its customers. Therefore, it gets easier to provide more valuable products and/or services to clients whilst lowering costs for maintenance, through Kaizen implementation. Additionally, when processes are improved, they reduce the number of defaults, defects, risks, unnecessary material usage, reworks, and errors.

Few ways Kaizen methodology can be applied include specific problems, strategic deployment, and total immersion. Kaizen can be applied to specific problems directly to bring about change. It can also be used in a strategic way to resolve issues in a business. An entire business can also implement Kaizen methodology via 'total immersion'.

In both strategic deployment and total immersion, Kaizen provides an understanding that is learned through action. This is often done through training and coaching that makes sure the desired results are reached. Once this training has been provided, it is possible for individuals to have the know-how in terms of applying these methods to other issues. The unique aspect of Kaizen is that it can be implemented on its own or added to pre-existing programs.

Kaizen methodology fundamentally requires a company's leadership team, middle management and all employees to collaborate and work in unison, consistently, to bring about small incremental improvements to its business process. Kaizen is a proactive technique i.e. employees are vigilant about the big and small problems faced by them at their workplace, and take pleasure it fixing issues collectively. Kaizen essentially requires teamwork. One of the more desirable aspects of Kaizen methodology is that it is an engaging, entertaining, stimulating and addictive approach.

Also, known as an "instant revolution", Kaizen is a quick methodology that can be applied in a much shorter time frame than other process improvement techniques.

Advantages of Kaizen

The term Kaizen comes from a Japanese phrase meaning "Make Better". It uses the Japanese judgment of improving the workplace internally to bring about desired results.

Kaizen can be implemented in a variety of ways, either to fix a specific problem or to change the entire structure of a business. Either way, it is a combination of minor improvements that end up having major profits. Common results of Kaizen include increased productivity, better quality, improved safety, quicker delivery, reduced costs and superior customer satisfaction.

It is also beneficial to the employees within a company. Companies that implement Kaizen methodology tend to have employees that enjoy what they do and find their work to be satisfying. Satisfied employees thus increase a company's productivity due to their own initiative and standard. Employees that are happy in their companies are also more loyal.

Kaizen methodology significantly lowers waste in many aspects of the company, including money, time, energy, production, area utilization, inventory, quality, employee retention and communications. It is typical for Kaizen to work on smaller problems of the company that ends up having a positive effect on larger problems. It is also one of the best and faster methods to achieve desired corporate goals.

Perhaps one of the most unique and interesting aspects about Kaizen is that it works directly with the employees and adds value to individuals, generally disregarded in most companies. Employees that are trained in the processes and feel like a valued member of a company are more willing to implement and speak out about positive changes and novel ideas. Those that have self-esteem and satisfaction with their jobs are more efficient and happy.

In Kaizen methodology, every single employee is involved and encouraged to look for problems they face within their role and department. They are asked to identify, analyze, review and solve problems to their best capability, which ends up having a profound effect on the company for a long time. Companies that have implemented Kaizen have received much more employee suggestions than companies that don't and most of these suggestions end up being applied.

The popular Lean methodology is known for its numerous benefits in terms of continuous improvement. However, there are some disadvantages that are worth noting as well. The most common disadvantage of Lean is that the entire organization needs to undergo a massive change. Successful implementation of Lean also needs a lot of time and resources. Lean therefore is conducive to large companies as against small or startups. All such limitations posed by 'Lean' are superbly overcome by Kaizen.

Kaizen helps in:

1. Time management.
2. Cost improvement.
3. Quality improvement.
4. Demand generation.
5. Demand fulfillment.
6. Support systems.

Here are some published statistics of successful Kaizen implementation in manufacturing-based industries-

- Production lead time reduced by 20 – 60 %

- Inventory level reduced by 20 – 70 %

- Inventory cost reduced by 30 – 70 %

- Productivity increased by 2 to 3-fold

- Space Utilization reduced by 10 – 40 %

- On Time Delivery improved to more than 95 %

- Capacity increased by 10 – 70 %

- Equipment Uptime enhanced up to 95 %

- Employee morale improved and turnover decreased.

Limitations of Kaizen

Kaizen methodology is growing in popularity. More and more companies around the globe are now opting for the strategic use of Kaizen. While there are many advantages of using Kaizen, there are some limitations that are worth being aware of, before deciding to implement it in your organization.

Sometimes, through Kaizen, it is necessary for companies to undergo a complete reset of their tactics and approach. Therefore, it can be quite difficult and cause an array of problems to the business if they are not ready or equipped to do so. It is necessary for companies to be very open to change as well as communicate in a constructive and open manner for Kaizen to be implemented correctly.

Since employees are a vital part of Kaizen's success, the company must foster an environment where employees are not scared to speak up or show signs of being territorial.

Another reason that Kaizen can be ineffective is that the new approach may, at first, be very inspiring and exciting but if the employees and company do not strive to maintain the tempo, the buzz can die down very quickly and cause all the changes to revert to their old ways. This can be very frustrating for the company that has invested time and money including this methodology to their business, only to have it short-lived. Also, it can deter companies from re-implementing Kaizen in a way that will work, due to a previous bad experience.

It can be difficult to get the ball rolling with Kaizen if the entire company, or the staff involved, are not aware of the benefits Kaizen offers.

Kaizen methodology requires work from the inside to have external results. It really comes down to effective and encouraging management; without which, it can be hard to get Kaizen off the ground.

Some employees may not want to undergo the necessary changes in their methods to see the advantages of Kaizen. Not everyone adjusts well to change too. So, it is important for everyone to have a clear understanding of Kaizen and the reasons for its implementation before the actual campaign begins. Like all improvement techniques, Kaizen will not have overnight success or see success for a while; therefore, the long-term goals must be clearly understood and accepted by everyone involved.

Change is constant ... Sometimes you Miss, Sometimes you Learn

Duality of Kaizen

Kaizen is intrinsically dual in nature. It is a union of 'Kaizen Philosophy' and 'Kaizen Action'.

- As a 'Philosophy', Kaizen is about developing organizational excellence by creating awareness. It is all about building a company-wide culture where all employees, senior management, and stakeholders are actively engaged in identifying and ideating ways of improving the business's performance, operations and processes.

- As 'Action', Kaizen is about organizing Kaizen events, workshops, focus groups and action force, dedicated to ideate and implement improvement plans to the company's existing processes, to make them better. Kaizen events are run by employee teams from all levels of the company, especially those most close to the process (being considered for improvement).

Kaizen works hand-in-glove with 'Lean' and 'Standardized work'. Lean shows ways of to eliminating waste, while standardized work captures the current best practices of a process. Thus, Kaizen campaigns have a broad scope, namely- to identify wastes, process inefficiencies, find ways to improve those inefficient processes and bring on desired change.

Tip: Standardized work includes cGMP prevailing in pharmaceutical, medical device and biotech industries. Since standardized work document continually evolves as process improvement happens, it is most *current* and a living document.

Kaizen Philosophies

When Kaizen is consistently applied as an 'action plan' through structured series of Kaizen events, it builds Kaizen culture i.e. Kaizen philosophy for that organization. The Kaizen 'philosophy' in turn propels further Kaizen 'action plans' and this cycle continues, to 'make processes better', endlessly ...

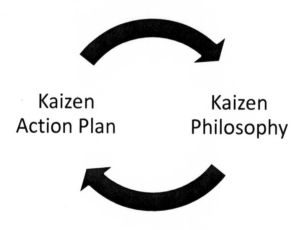

Kaizen
Action Plan

Kaizen
Philosophy

Kaizen philosophy inspires and motivates employees to think creatively about their work i.e. work to create a difference. Continuous application of 'Kaizen philosophy' to an 'action plan', thus creates a stupendous and far-reaching value, by building an effective culture of continuing improvement.

Kaizen is based on the philosophical belief that everything can be improved! Some organizations look at a process and see 'it as running fine' while organizations that follow Kaizen see a process 'that can be improved'

Processes never stay in status quo in a Kaizen facility- small changes to make things better, happen consistently. Kaizen involves small work teams that bring about small changes, that sum up to BIG substantial changes over a long term. Kaizen is also a gentle, employee-friendly technique to bring on a BIG change in business environment, culture, outlook and output.

Kaizen helps meet both Manufacturing and Corporate goals such as:

Corporate goals:

- Improve cash-flow management.
- Increase top line and bottom line numbers.
- Reduce costs.
- Improve revenues.
- Reduce and mitigate risks.
- Improve competitive advantage.
- Enhance workspace utilization.
- Eliminate waste and hard work.
- Use tools to maximize business efficiency and automation.
- Speed new product development and market launches.

- Improve vendor relationship management.
- Maintain questioning, open-minded approvals for continual improvement.
- Motivate employees for cooperation & collaboration.
- Reduce inventory both stocks and work-in-progress.
- Improve workplace quality.
- Improve product QA (Quality Assurance).

Manufacturing goals:

- Achieve maximum quality with maximum efficiency.
- Shorten production lines and effective line balancing.
- Reduce machine downtime.
- Improve productivity.
- Shorten lead times (Throughput times).
- Meet production demands.
- Meet delivery schedules.
- Comply EHS (Environment, Health, Safety), FDA (Food Drug Administration), cGMP (*current* Good Manufacturing Practices), cGAMP (*current* Good Automated Manufacturing Practices), cGCP (*current* Good Clinical Practices) and other applicable regulations.

Kaizen starts with a problem; more precisely the recognition that a problem exists!

24

If there is no problem, there is no potential for improvement...

Conventional Wisdom	Kaizen Philosophy
Higher quality leads to higher costs	Higher quality leads to lower costs
Larger lots lead to lower costs	Smaller lots lead to lower costs
Workers do not need to be considered	A 'Thinking' worker is a 'Productive' worker

Characteristics of Kaizen:

- A plan that addresses and incorporates the above essential ingredients.
- An approach that addresses the key issues simultaneously rather than in a linear sequence.
- A resource plan that is broad in scope.

Improvements through Kaizen have a process-focus via people-efforts. Kaizen philosophy prescribes that mistakes, errors or problems happen at work, due to fault of the system and not the worker. Hence, all problem-solving solutions must be targeted to change the system and not change the worker. Workers must be job trained and also about their fit into the company, how they contribute and the impact each worker's input has on the business's overall performance.

The philosophy of Kaizen, which simply means 'make better' needs to be adopted by any organization seeking to implement Lean improvements that go beyond cost-cutting. Kaizen events are opportunities to make focused changes in the workplace.

Conventional approach	Kaizen approach
Employees are the problem	Process is the problem
Doing my job	Helping to get things done
Understanding my job	Knowing how my job fits in the process
Measure individual's performance	Measure process performance
Change the person	Change the process
Correct errors	Reduce errors and variations
Who made the error?	What allowed the error to happen?

Organizational Excellence

Customer Delight and Loyalty

Improve Speed, Quality, Workflow and Revenue

Train and Motivate Workforce

Continuous Improvement: Daily Kaizen and Blitz Kaizen

Value Stream Mapping and Muda (Waste) Identification

Voice of Customer: Customer- Defined Value

HOUSE OF KAIZEN

Kaizen philosophy brings about open-ness at workplace. It also makes everyone aware of their duties and responsibilities. In a Kaizen facility, the senior leadership is expected to focus on business strategies, create proactive solutions and provide tools of the trade to Kaizen's action force. While, the Kaizen action force has complete responsibility and accountability to bring Kaizen in action, improve revenue through Kaizen efforts. There is no micro-management.

Further, trust is built and transparency becomes a way of work life. Rather than shoving problems under the carpet, issues are discussed openly, the blame game ends; communication improves; everyone works together to solve problems rather than being concerned about their own piece. And most importantly, customers take their rightful place in an organization's psyche; Voice of the customer gets heard ...

3 pillars of Kaizen

✓ Housekeeping.

✓ Waste elimination.

✓ Standardization.

The House of Kaizen stays on three pillars- good housekeeping, effective waste-elimination and efficient standardization of work. These pillars are cemented strong with 3 factors- visual management, Kaizen leader and Kaizen training. This 3x3 formula is a basic necessity for success with Kaizen.

27

Ten basic requirements for improvement via Kaizen

1. Throw out all fixed ideas about how to do things.

2. Visualize how new process will work Vs how it will not work.

3. Say 'No' to excuses. Say 'No' to accept status quo.

4. Don't seek perfection. Initially, go for 80/20 Pareto's rule.

5. Correct errors immediately.

6. Be frugal on spending on improvements.

7. Be creative with your improvement efforts.

8. Find root cause before attempting change or improvement.

9. Solicit views across the organization. Change needs every employee's ownership. It is not a one-person show.

10. Improvement is a continuous phenomenon.

"An open mind leaves a chance for someone to drop a worthwhile thought in it"– Mark Twain

---

Take-a-Five

Take five minutes to think about these questions and to write down your answers:

- What continuous improvement activities have you done in your company?

- Can you think of one thing you could change that would improve the way you do your operations or tasks?

Kaizen Principles

Kaizen improvement is based on EIGHT guiding principles:

1. 'Good' process changes bring 'Great' results-Published statistics indicate that, as much as 35% waste gets generated in a manufacturing facility. A job done right first time, produces less waste. Thus, eliminating this waste, profits rise.

2. Go see for yourself (the Gemba) to grasp the current situation.

3. Employees are more likely to accept gradual changes than drastic complete overhauls. It is vital that everyone in the company believes 'change is good' and is necessary for the company's survival.

4. No Rigidity or making excuses. *"We have always done it this way and don't see why*

we must change now" mindset is unacceptable. The company's senior leadership must provide complete information about benefits of Kaizen to all its employees. Effective employee counseling must be done whenever necessary. It must be emphasized that Kaizen methodology is one of the tools, the company is using to survive, grow and keep it running under the challenging market economy hardships. No Kaizen might result in- No Company, thus No Jobs!

5. Speak with data, manage by facts.

6. Act to contain and correct root causes of problems.

7. Collaboration is crucial, work as a team. It helps also encourages employees to take ownership for their work, enhances morale and motivation.

8. Kaizen is everybody's business.

Use Kaizen to develop people, creativity, innovation, competitive edge in products and services. Shape & spread ideas... bring a turnaround!

Kaizen Rules

The following three rules are commonly prescribed to ensure Kaizen mindset is being followed and that every individual's creativity is being fully utilized:

1. Spend no or less money.

2. Add no staff.

3. Add no/less workspace or machines.

Kaizen comprises of a bunch of smaller tools such as- 5S, Kanban, Visual management etc. in its kit. The picture below of Kaizen umbrella depicts few such important tools of Kaizen.

5S

Kanban

Zero Defect

Just-in-time (JIT)

Small Team Activity

Root Cause Analysis

Productivity Improvement

Quality/ Ops Improvement

Robotics

Voice of Customer (VOC)

Empowered Workforce

Visual Management

SMEDS (Reduce changeovers)

Suggestion Systems (Kaizen cards)

Total Quality Management (TQM)

Total Productive Maintenance (TPM)

Typical Results of Kaizen:

Up to 45% improvement in throughput time (lead-time), 50% reduction is manufacturing space utilization and 65% reduction in work-in-process, have been observed with Kaizen implementation in manufacturing -based companies, across various industry verticals.

Kaizen is a continuing improvement cycle i.e. as soon as existing set of problems are resolved, new problems that might show up are fixed appropriately and consistently, thus making the production systems very robust.

Plan- Do- Check- Act (PDCA) Cycle

This cycle is based on the scientific method of inquiry. The PDCA Cycle is driven by suggestions, and the suggestions come from everyone who has a stake in the success of the company.

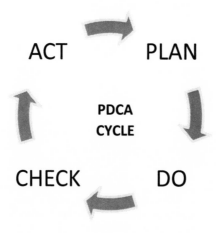

One of the most notable features of Kaizen is that big results come from many small changes accumulated over time. However, this has been misunderstood to mean that Kaizen equals small changes. In fact, Kaizen means everyone is involved in making improvements. Just as a journey of thousand miles begins with a small step, the same is true with Kaizen. While most changes are small, the practice of 'making small change' is done consistently, leading to illustrious results.

Take-a-Five

Take five minutes to think about these questions and to write down your answer:

Q: How will Kaizen change activities you're presently doing at your workplace?

Tip: If your company has not been into continuous improvement, this will be a big change for you in many ways. You will need time to think about what you do, and time to learn and discover ways to do what you do better. You will need tools to capture and record your improvement ideas- be it a notepad or digital apps such as Evernote, One Note, and several others. The key is to understand the relationship of your work with regards to everyone else's, within the 'value stream' of your organization.

Tip: Purpose of Kaizen: Kaizen activities focus on each *process* and every *operation* to add *value* and eliminate *waste*. I will elaborate on the terms 'value' and 'waste' in forthcoming chapters.

Tip: Difference between Kaizen and Continuous Improvement: Kaizen is a methodology; Continuous Improvement is the process to bring results of Kaizen.

You have to keep working hard just to stay in the same place and even harder if you are to make progress

---

When to Introduce Kaizen at your Workplace?

Before learning when, let us first understand why to apply Kaizen in the pharmaceutical, medical device, and biotech companies.

'The only purpose of a business is, to make a satisfied customer' applies to life sciences business too. And, Kaizen can be immediately employed to impact one or all three measures for these businesses- throughput (cycle time), product/ process cost and customer satisfaction.

Depending on the demographics, a pharmaceutical company's business environment and customers vary. Customers could be doctors, patients, caregivers, insurance companies, regulatory agencies etc. For prescription medicines and most devices, the prescribing doctor is the actual customer, while for OTC medicines the patient or caregiver is the likely customer.

These industries are highly controlled. Elaborate good manufacturing practices are in place to ensure only safe and efficacious medicines/devices are launched in the market. The process of drug discovery research, product development, clinical studies and approvals pose additional challenges to the industry's inherent problems, such as- increasing customer needs, changing regulations and see-sawing socio-economic policies. Under the circumstances, how can pharmaceutical, device or biotech companies thrive, excel and grow?

It has been observed that, pharmaceutical industry typically exhibits following statistics:

- Finished goods inventory: 60 – 90 days
- Labor value-add time: 15-25%
- Annual productivity improvement: 1-5%
- Zero defect rate: 65-80%
- Number of suppliers: 10-55
- Low first-pass-yield.
- Sub-optimal equipment performance i.e. around 10 to 60% Overall Equipment Effectiveness (OEE).
- High changeover times.
- Long production lead times. Production lead time delays: 120-180 days.

High inventories, changing disease situations for example a new strain of virus affecting population, drug-product pricing pressures, daily firefighting scenarios at production lines, increasing costs of running operations, rising competition (including those from generics), changing regulations, country specific approval procedures, losses in sales due to expiring patents, etc. are additional hurdles faced by organizations in the life sciences sector.

Pharmaceuticals industry requires a paradigm shift to deal with the above challenges!

I can emphatically state that many a times for sinking as well as growing businesses, Kaizen becomes the backbone of a successful business transformation. In course of my working with several pharmaceutical companies globally, I have observed a direct correlation between Kaizen implementation and a business's profit figures. Overhead expenses nosedive with Kaizen process improvement.

Today, pharmaceutical manufacturing has an un-met need of better capacity utilization coupled with lower overhead costs, and Kaizen effectively fulfills this niche! Rigorous Kaizen-ing have resulted in fantastic profits.

Kaizen may be used both in technical as well as non-technical process improvements and their validations. The technical processes encompass- R&D, manufacturing, quality control, quality assurance, regulatory, scale-up & validation.

While, the non-technical processes include-procurement, finance, IT, Human Resources, corporate governance, marketing & sales, logistics & supply chain, mergers & acquisitions, business expansions, business transformation. Few examples are-

- Crisis stabilization & control: Finance restructuring, improving cash-flow, asset reduction, stakeholder communications, change of CEO or senior leadership team.
- New Leadership: Change of CEO or senior leadership team.
- Strategic Focus: Redefine core business, downsizing, outsourcing, marketing & sales.
- Organizational Change: Structural changes, key people changes, new hires etc.
- Critical process improvement: Quality improvement, marketing & sales improvement, research- product development- operations-logistics, information & system control.

Kaizen methods can be applied not only to manufacturing but also to service processes, facility realty of pharmaceutical, device and biotech businesses, including streamlining administration workflow.

The best part of Kaizen is that you don't always need to hire an external consultant. A leader can emerge from within the company and steer the workforce from top to bottom to work in unison, seamlessly to improve business efficiency.

While this sounds simple and straightforward, from an execution point of view it requires great efforts, teamwork from both workers and managers to get comfortable with this new method of working.

> *"If you don't have time to do it right, you must have time to do it over"* - *Anonymous*

In Kaizen, workers lead the change efforts, managers might be in the supporting role. The Kaizen task force collaborates with everyone within the organization to seek out problems, possible solution ideas of improvement, as well as obtain consensus on potential decisions. Action happens immediately sans hours of analysis-paralysis on shop floor of a Kaizen facility. Since changes are small and incremental in scope, individual mistakes are easily rectified without any fuss. Also, as changes are made briskly and in quick succession, results are seen in few days, a week or two.

Pharmaceutical industry globally uses highly sophisticated machines for manufacturing and latest technology for marketing and selling their products. They reach customers in several different ways; educating them about product features and potential health benefits. It is also true that customer of today is well-informed as compared to a customer of yester years.

Hence, having efficient processes gets extremely important. For example, Flow- does it work? What are the activities? Do activities when strung in a sequence add value? How are decisions made? Who makes them? How do decision impacts get measured? Additionally, markets change, technology changes, customers change, business problems change continually. If a company considers customer–problem–solutions to be something static or given, and it prepares itself for a ride—downwards.

Organizations gain a sustained long-term performance advantage by:

- Creating robust process design and built-in quality (i.e. quality-by-design).

- Implementing Single-Minute Exchange of Dies (SMEDS) to reduce changeover times and maintain optimal batch sizes.

- Initiating Total Productive Maintenance (TPM) to improve equipment performance.

- Employing 'Pull Production' and 'Just-In-Time (JIT) Production & Logistics' to reduce throughput times and inventories.

- Engaging people in daily problem-solving leading to a culture of continual improvement in the organization.

Kaizen implementation in companies has realized following ball-park payoffs:

- Inventory reduction: 90%
- Productivity improvement: 100%

- Defects decreased: 100%
- Throughput time reduced: 90%
- Manufacturing costs reduced: 35%
- Floor space reduced: 55%

Unfortunately, very few pharmaceutical companies are aware of these opportunities!

An economic or revenue slowdown is by far an apt time to introduce reforms via Kaizen.

Difficult times tend to pave way for radical changes, employees are more receptive to change ideas, open to Kaizen practice and eager to help out with Kaizen campaigns.

A planned schedule of future Kaizen events can also become part of a control plan to ensure that operations, systems adopt a continual improvement approach with appropriate metrics, to ongoing process management. Example if Kaizen is being used to help 5S an area, an operator's movement (as distance traveled by steps) could be selected as metric.

Tip: A word of caution- if Kaizen is used as a ploy to layoff workers, employees will see through the scheme and the Kaizen cookie will crumble A basic level of trust between company's senior leadership and employees is a must for Kaizen to succeed.

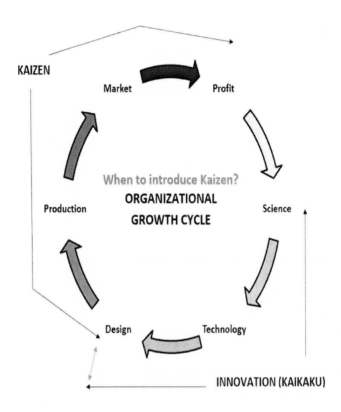

Myth: We are a highly-regulated industry. All product dossiers are registered. Any change due to Kaizen will involve repeat bioavailability and/or clinical studies.

Fact: Kaizen can be included in 'Design space' for all technical processes during development via QbD. There is absolutely no cause for added expenses viz. refiling/ resubmission or scale-up and post approval change (SUPAC).

Myth: We are cGMP facility bound by USFDA and other strict regulations. Kaizen is not for us.

Fact: Kaizen works hand-in-hand with cGMP and all regulations. In addition, Kaizen improves processes and reduces costs by 5-50%; which translates into an equivalent amount of profit.

Myth: Kaizen involves too much data generation; which adds to product cost making its sales challenging.

Fact: Kaizen can be included at any stage of a process's or product's lifecycle at meager cost. Similarly, data generated for Kaizen implementation is minimal when compared with Six Sigma or such other methodologies. However, Kaizen implementation gives far reaching benefits as much as Six sigma in many cases.

A brief pause...

Although Kaizen originated in Japan it has received glory worldwide. Kicking-off its journey in Toyota company, Kaizen has benefited the automobile sector, although it can be implemented across any industry vertical.

Pharmaceutical, medical device, and biotech companies follow the state-of-the-art Good Manufacturing Practices (GMP), they still don't hold the 'Quality Crown'. Rising number of 483 letters to pharmaceutical companies indicates that there is a large room for improvement.

Kaizen is a mix of 'action plan' and 'philosophy'.

Continuously applying Kaizen philosophy as an action plan, ingrains Kaizen methodology into a business process, consequently making the business profitable and self-sustaining despite tough competition or a see-sawing economy.

"We are what we repeatedly do. Excellence, therefore, is not an act, but a habit"- Aristotle

Take-a-Five

Now that we have completed this chapter, take five minutes to think about these questions and to write down your answers:

- What did you learn from reading this chapter that stands out as particularly useful or interesting?

- Do you have any questions about the topics presented in this chapter? If so, what are they?

- What additional information do you need to fully understand the ideas presented in this chapter?

Coming Up: In the next chapter, we will discuss various types of Kaizen ...

Chapter 2: Types of Kaizen

In this chapter, we will see ...

- ✓ Lean Kaizen

- ✓ Gemba Kaizen

- ✓ Personal Kaizen

- ✓ Modular Kaizen

- ✓ Flow Kaizen

- ✓ Process Kaizen

- ✓ Agile Kaizen

- ✓ Blitz Kaizen

- ✓ Daily Kaizen

Shruti Bhat

Lean Kaizen

Lean Kaizen is a continuous improvement methodology to get rid of excess waste involved in a process. Lean identifies waste as- Muda (waste in manufacturing system), muri (waste due to overburden) and mura (waste created due to unevenness of workloads). Kaizen is the foundation of Lean methods of production and focuses largely on reducing, or eliminating waste, increasing productivity and attaining continual improvement relating to organization's methods.

Lean Kaizen incorporates Kaizen's ideas of continual improvement and focuses on making/ applying small changes for a significant amount of time, to achieve desired results. This method involves all types of employees at different levels within the company and requires complete involvement by everyone, to allow anyone to speak up regarding problems and ways of improvement.

The main technique often used here involves analytical aspect and includes methods such as '5-Whys' and 'Ishikawaka' to pinpoint ways of reducing waste in certain areas of production. A Kaizen implementation plan is then designed, which is often applied almost immediately. The solutions involved are typically minute and more solutions are added as problems arise.

It is necessary to assess and follow-up on the actions for improvement, to be able to analyze how well the plan is working and to make sure that it continues to be applied for a long period. The system of Kaizen allows all employees to have a say in decision-making and boosts employee morale within a company. Since this method is continuous in action, employees can choose to speak up on issues when they occur – which allows for solutions to make a significant impact. Therefore, solutions via Lean Kaizen methodology are absolutely customized to the type of problems occurring in a section or department. Hence, Lean Kaizen creates a customized solution not only specific to an industry segment but the company-specific too.

Though Kaizen does appear to focus on fixing manufacturing process related problems, it is also used to improve the organization as a whole. Hence, Lean Kaizen plays a critical role in overall business process improvement.

Anything that positively contributes to the safety, efficiency or productivity of the organization is greatly valued in this methodology. While employees can come up with ideas at their own leisure, it is often encouraged by organizations to arrange brainstorming sessions on a regular basis. Typically, in a brainstorming session, employees are given a topic to focus on and discuss possibilities of improvement regarding the given subject.

It is most effective for these brainstorming or Kaizen, sessions to include around five to seven people. The numbers vary on the company size, markets of operation, employee strength, number, frequency and magnitude of problems etc. Organizations targeting improvement via Lean Kaizen should generally allow for employees that are involved in the session to have some time off during their work day to come up with solutions. The reason Kaizen sessions work well is because different viewpoints are heard and can help bring about a solution that works for all.

The spirit of Lean Kaizen is that 'no single day should pass by an organization without some type of small improvement being done in some process within the company-
Unknown

Lean Kaizen is extremely difficult to implement in life sciences companies as Lean advocates small batch sizes. Improper use of Lean Kaizen on a pharmaceutical company shop floor, produces poor operational output. For example- small batch sizes may mean higher percentage of granules wasted on a high-speed tablet-press, while working on low speed tablet machines would directly impact productivity negatively.

Implementing 'one piece flow' i.e. a process in which each product moves through the production process, one unit at a time, is difficult to implement in the traditional pharmaceutical manufacture of capsules, tablets and other dosage forms. One piece flow might, however, work with additive manufacturing i.e. 3D printing.

Furthermore, pharmaceutical (and device) manufacturing requires meticulous cleaning and line clearance between batches, unless it is a dedicated line for a product. To avoid line clearance procedures for dedicated lines, batches must have same blend compositions and products be dose-proportionate. What that means is- if a tableting line produces Product A having multiple strengths 100 mg, 150 mg, 200 mg and 300 mg, then batch of 100 mg label claim must be manufactured first, followed by others in ascending chronology.

In all other scenarios, such as, non-dedicated lines, different blend compositions and/or non-dose-proportionate products, obtaining line clearance between batches is a must. This stipulation disallows quick changeovers on the shop floor. For example, a clean-in-place process may require a full day and line clearance may not be received as test results may not be available to QA. Such incidences usually happen since line clearance tests are complex and take time. For example- if a microbiology study is involved, line clearance test results may get delayed by 5-15 days!

Lean manufacturing technique cannot be applied as-is to pharmaceutical Ops. However, Lean principles combined with Kaizen philosophy can be applied to improve pharmaceutical operational productivity, control WIP, reduce cycle times, variations and enhance process efficiency.

Pharmaceutical manufacturing is a complex process therefore, improvement teams require a variety of skills.

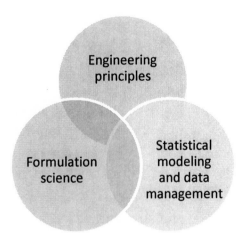

Few modes where improvement via Lean Kaizen is extremely helpful:

- ✓ Little or no leadership from top management.
- ✓ Infrequent management reviews.
- ✓ Top talent not used.
- ✓ Poor support for finance, IT, maintenance team, Human Resources.
- ✓ The focus is on training, not improvement.
- ✓ Poor communication of initiatives and progress.
- ✓ Lack of appropriate recognition and reward.
- ✓ Projects not tied to business goals.
- ✓ Poorly defined project goals, scope, and metrics.
- ✓ Wrong project teams.
- ✓ Infrequent team meetings.

Benefits of Lean Kaizen

Lean Kaizen methodology involves making small changes within an organization and implementing these changes on a continuous basis. These improvements allow organizations to reduce waste and improve productivity. The method involves all workers of the company and allows for everyone to have a say regarding possibilities of improvement, as well as pinpointing methods that are not efficient or could be made better. Unlike workshops that take place annually or monthly, Lean Kaizen is implemented regularly and continuously.

The ideas that are addressed in Lean Kaizen are often small since this method works effectively when small changes are made. These small changes tend to improve important aspects of the company such as efficiency, safety, and productiveness. Aside from working on aspects that are deemed problematic within a process, Lean Kaizen also encourages workers to speak up regarding all aspects of improvement.

The best advantage of Lean Kaizen is that it greatly reduces waste. This can include waste from transportation, supply chain logistics, skills, inventory, processes, and production. It also lowers costs, increases safety, allows for more efficient delivery and improves customer satisfaction.

Another advantage of implementing Lean Kaizen is that it creates a lot of clutter-free space due to the elimination of unnecessary items. It also increases the quality of the product, uses assets in a better manner, improves communication and allows employees to feel valued in the company. Since employees are a significant part of the Kaizen campaign, they feel empowered and contribute to the organization's cause in a big way and tends to augment their loyalty and dedication.

Employees that are continuously assessing their environment to find methods of improvement have a higher chance of addressing necessary changes within the workspace. Since employees that are involved tend to have higher morale, they work more effectively and experience more job satisfaction.

Since Lean Kaizen focuses on making small changes, the results are immediate. When an organization chooses to undergo large changes, it takes much more time to see results and there may be several negative drawbacks as well.

The advantage of using Lean Kaizen is that it can work on a large number of small problems, which bring about BIG results.

It is still necessary for companies to undergo large changes for certain projects however, Lean Kaizen has a positive effect on the entire process by making it easier to implement in increments and to analyze detailed aspects as well as the *bigger picture.*

The reason Lean Kaizen is widely used and favored is because, it is a continuous method that continually makes little improvements, that greatly improve the processes of an organization and lowers waste.

"Lean is a principle, Kaizen is a process. The traditional Lean methodology will not work for pharmaceuticals; more so for the continuous manufacturing process. Lean Kaizen is a Kaizen-based process to achieve Lean.

Hence, Lean Kaizen deals with waste elimination. Lean may be achieved by fourteen different ways including Toyota production systems (TPS), Theory of constraints (TOC), Heijunka, Kanban and so on...

The choice depends on company's size and departmental activities. Even a start-up can use Kaizen to achieve Lean, that is the beauty of Kaizen"

- Dr. Shruti U. Bhat

Lean Kaizen is used by life sciences companies throughout the world and continues to work well for organizations of all sizes and segments. However, it is good to be aware of the limitations of Lean Kaizen before implementing this method to your organization.

Limitations of Lean Kaizen

A large drawback of Lean Kaizen is that it requires organizations to change their governance style and communication methods. It can be hard for companies that are used to working in a certain way, to suddenly make changes to their work style. For Lean Kaizen to take off the ground, companies must allow open communication and empower employees to speak up on issues around their workplace. Lean Kaizen will not work at all sans transparent dialogues between everyone in the workplace.

Another limitation noted in Lean Kaizen is that this method focuses largely on reducing waste, which can withdraw focus from other important aspects. Change management procedures must be extremely efficient to make Lean Kaizen campaign a success.

Usually implementing Lean Kaizen has a positive spin on employees (since they are valued), however, it can rake-up fear of losing their jobs or may feel threatened because changes at workplace might displace them from their 'comfort zone'.

It is necessary for all employees to be well-informed and aware of the *real* reasons for implementing Lean Kaizen. Otherwise, the drive that motivated workers during the initial stages can dwindle down over time. This is especially harmful if the solutions have not yet been put to action. The organization will not receive the desired results and can deter employees from wanting to continuously use Kaizen strategy.

Implementing Lean Kaizen can be quite stressful since it becomes a new focal point within the organization. It can cause the work area to become more detached and objective since employees may feel continuous pressure to exceed their prior performances. If stress levels in workers become too high, then it can have a negative effect on both efficiency and productivity of the workforce.

Lean Kaizen can be applied for process improvement in all departments within the pharmaceutical, medical device, and biotech industries.

Gemba Kaizen

Gemba (aka Genba) in Japanese means "real place", which refers to the actual place of action or a place where 'value' is created. This method is typically used to add 'activities of value' that help increase customer satisfaction and business growth.

In Gemba Kaizen, when an error occurs, it is necessary to deal with the issue right away. For example, if a machine is not working, then it must be fixed immediately. If a customer is upset, then the situation must be fixed as soon as possible. Such 'immediate' solutions will naturally be stop-gap arrangements and may not get to the root of the problem. However, with Gemba Kaizen, such matters remain open until closed, after getting to the bottom of the issue and resolving it permanently. Gemba Kaizen encourages the asking of "Why" for such situations to bring about successful and sustainable result.

After the cause of the problem has been identified and a solution has been designed, it must be shared with everyone. Sharing of ideas about how to handle or how to stop such and/or similar error from re-occurring is critical.

Gemba Kaizen typically uses two methods of solving problems:

The first approach involves innovation by using the best technology to solve problems, hence is the most expensive option.

The second approach employs common tools, and a variety of blended techniques, that don't require large sums of money.

The main aspect of implementing Gemba Kaizen involves 'standardization', 'housekeeping' along with 'Muda elimination'.

'Standardization' is defined as the most effective way of handling a job or issue. The 'standard' is continuously maintained in a certain fashion to bring about products (and services) with consistent quality. This also helps eliminate defects, reworks, and problems from happening again.

'Housekeeping' is a necessary factor for effective management. It requires workers to be aware of their environment and to practice desired methods of housekeeping. It is necessary to teach employees how to have self-discipline to provide adequate customer satisfaction.

'Muda' is the Japanese word for waste and applies to activities that add no 'value' to the process.

Muda elimination focuses on getting rid of redundant resources such as- time, systems, procedures, facilities, employees, materials or machinery, business verticals etc. which do not provide any value to the organization. It is an effective way of reducing costs and is also beneficial to the overall productivity within an organization.

The most common types of waste found in organizations involve- transportation, inventory, supply chain logistics, rejects, overproduction, waiting, machine idle times etc. We shall cover this aspect in greater detail in the forthcoming chapters.

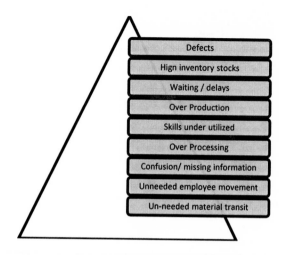

9 Mudas (Wastes found in For-profit or Non-profit organizations

Benefits of Gemba Kaizen

Using Gemba Kaizen methodology in an organization helps in a variety of ways as it deals directly with a problem when it occurs.

Gemba Kaizen is one of the commonly used methodologies to improving an organization's procedures and increasing customer satisfaction. Gemba Kaizen helps to lower overall costs and improve productivity. It also has a positive effect on all employees of the company and allows for individuals to feel that their contributions are meaningful, truly valued and appreciated. Employees who feel that they have a say in decisions and their voices are heard, tend to have a greater sense of self-esteem, responsibility, accountability and give better output.

Gemba Kaizen is also beneficial because it gives all workers a voice and allows them to come up with creative and value-driven solutions. Everyone are directly involved in coming up with methods of improvement and this allows for increased productivity, collaboration, teamwork, employee morale, and motivation.

Traditionally, Kaizen creates a sense of employee loyalty to the company, but in today's time's employee loyalty is a vestigial virtue- not present in the workforce and not valued by companies!

Gemba Kaizen also implements ideas used in Lean manufacturing, which helps to reduce waste, unnecessary procedures and resources. The elimination of non-value added activities helps to lower overall costs in an organization. Moreover, when waste is eliminated it allows for all employees to contribute in a more productive way that helps to raise their performance levels.

It is necessary to perform continuous monitoring after Gemba Kaizen is implemented to track, analyze, manage and sustain the changes involved. Whenever needed, the workforce must be re-structured appropriately to other areas of business.

One of the main goals for Gemba Kaizen is to eliminate anything that is not valuable, or adds value, to an organization, whether it is systems, procedures, employees, business verticals, machinery, facility etc.

This method can be performed individually once employees are aware, understand the method and reasons for Gemba Kaizen. Some organizations that use Gemba Kaizen tend to frequently perform work groups that help employees to brainstorm and come up with well-rounded and creative solutions.

Gemba Kaizen is usually implemented by dealing with problems directly at the source. The process involves educating the entire workforce on methods of analyzing and observing issues within an organization and coming up with improvement solutions. It encourages employees to be aware of various issues and to recommend suggestions for improvement.

Once a solution is determined, it is implemented and monitored to track its success. If a desirable result is reached, then the solution is passed on for use if the issue reoccurs. Typically, Gemba Kaizen prevents the same problems from reoccurring.

Limitations of Gemba Kaizen

One of the profound tasks to do for Gemba Kaizen technique to succeed in a company is to encourage and monitor methods of communication and select right candidates to oversee this important step.

One of the most significant limitations of Gemba Kaizen worth considering are the costs involved in identifying errors and root causes for the same. Often, this needs strong supervision, analysis and micro-management of the company's various business processes. It is also necessary for managers to be able to listen to employees and to help with the various stages involved in applying solutions. Thus, there must be an open communication channel within the organization.

Gemba Kaizen may be applied for process improvement in all departments within the pharmaceutical, medical device, and biotech industries.

Note: *What are the differences between Kaizen, Lean Kaizen, and Gemba Kaizen?*

While Kaizen, Lean Kaizen, and Gemba Kaizen all involve improving an organization, there are some differences that make these different methods desirable to various organizations.

Unlike Gemba Kaizen and Lean Kaizen, Kaizen itself can be applied to all aspects of one's life, including work, personal and social aspects. In terms of a workforce, Kaizen strives to make small changes on a continuing basis, which eventually has a large effect on the company in a positive manner.

Lean Kaizen deals with eliminating process wastes. On the other hand, Gemba Kaizen is typically viewed as a method that strives to solve problems as they occur, in a timely and productive manner. Gemba Kaizen is often thought of as the most effective method of the three due to its focus on 'results'.

For Gemba Kaizen to be successful, the root of the problem must be identified and a solution should be implemented as soon as possible. Once a desirable solution is reached, the method of solving the problem is shared with everyone in the company to prevent the same problem from re-occurring.

Gemba 'Go and see' approach encourages leaders, managers, and supervisors to walk out to the work area to solve problems and apply specific applications.

All these methods can be performed individually as well as in groups. For any of these methods to be successful, there needs to be open communication between all members of the organization alongside constant monitoring. Aside from increasing productivity, customer satisfaction and reducing waste, Kaizen, Lean Kaizen and Gemba Kaizen all help raise employee morale.

Myth: Kaizen can interfere with Quality Management Systems (QMS) of the manufacturing facility.

Fact: This is not true. Kaizen is very much part of QMS.

Personal Kaizen

Personal Kaizen encompasses everything an individual does or can do, to continuously improve their work, relationships, health, mind to bring joy and success into their work and life. Since we are part of a society or a community, our actions impact those around us. Hence, Personal Kaizen although indirectly, brings about improvement in the community.

Charity begins at home is a popular adage in England. It essentially implies is 'change begins with you, the person'.

Self-starter individuals initiate Personal Kaizen by themselves. Those in need of support can be helped by their Managers/Supervisors. Create small improvement teams, help co-workers identify problems in the work you do together, discover better ways of working as a team and improve the work environment.

How Does Personal Kaizen Benefit You?

Personal Kaizen helps eliminate wasted motion, transit, delays and bureaucracy in work, so that, one can do what one does best with ease, clarity and focus. It provides methods for you to think about what you do and how can you contribute ideas that benefit not just yourself, but also the entire company or community simultaneously.

Personal Kaizen helps ego and conflict management. Thus, it is a great tool for Human Resources manager and budding leaders.

Modular Kaizen

Modular Kaizen is a business process improvement tool that aims to stop panic when a problem arises.

Modular Kaizen is a type of business improvement methodology that allows for continuous improvement to take place in an environment that experiences frequent disruption or interruptions. It is a modified version of the standard Kaizen process and is designed to bring about fast results. Unlike standard Kaizen, Modular Kaizen does not distract key employees (such as managers and operators) from their regular duties until it is necessary.

Tip: Kaizen events (discussed later in this book), otherwise known as Kaizen Blitz, are notorious for stealing key players from their vital roles to have them participate in building solutions. However, Modular Kaizen requires the involvement of participants for short periods of time through various activities, which still allow for the regular workflow to continue. It is the antithesis of Kaizen Blitz and does not require each team member to be present in a sole setting until a solution has been determined. Instead, it takes place over small meetings in increments.

Modular Kaizen works well with other process methods such as DMAIC (Define-Measure-Analyze-Improve-Control) and PDCA models.

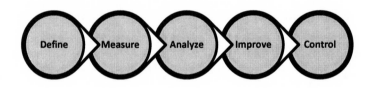

Moreover, Modular Kaizen can be used simultaneously with other business improvement methods such as ISO, Balanced Score Card.

Lowering disruptions is an intrinsic feature of Modular Kaizen. The action isn't required until each stage has been checked and evaluated, which requires analyzing data and making sure that the solution is applicable to current processes. Modular Kaizen doesn't encourage panic response to a problem. In fact, it encourages things to calm down and settle before coming up with a plan to implement changes.

Modular Kaizen uses many of the traditional Lean manufacturing tools but slightly modifies them to make it more applicable to working environments. The main tools of Modular Kaizen are created to figure out the current performance level, figure out where and what the disruptions are and to lower, or completely get rid of, waste that does not contribute to the flow efficiency within a process or operation.

Value Stream Mapping is an important tool used in Modular Kaizen. It offers a way to identify areas generating waste and makes them efficient. Other tools used in Modular Kaizen campaigns include: 5S system, disruption identification, 8 wastes, tri-metric matrix, project management, error proofing, CAPA, quality at the source, process control, fast transition, pull technology, modular flow, and daily work management.

The first stage of Modular Kaizen is to 'Check'. The 'check' stage focuses on the exact areas that are being disrupted. This deals with investigation and understanding the reason for disruption. It is assessed to see if the disruption happened due to special circumstances and aims to find out who and what caused the disruption. It is also evaluated to check the urgency of the matter. The timeline of the disruption is documented as well.

The next stage after check is to 'Act'. While it may seem counterintuitive, Modular Kaizen recommends monitoring the situation and to refrain from action until appropriate monitoring has taken place. After monitoring, it is time to investigate by assigning a team to have an in-depth look at the disruption and to report their findings. 'Act' stage calls for processes to be updated and standardized for using them effectively and efficiently. No actions take place until the first stage of checking is complete.

During the "Do" stage, ideas of improvement are tested using a variety of tools. This helps figure out which resource would be ideal for the situation, while testing it out in a time frame that is more desirable.

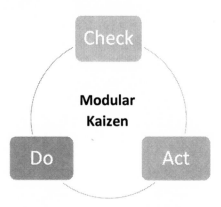

While the overall goal of Modular Kaizen is like Kaizen Blitz and incorporates many of the same components, Modular Kaizen makes sure to schedule many smaller events to allow individuals to continue with their regular work. This makes it ideal for implementing at any given stage of a process since its effects will not be as drastic as standard Kaizen.

Modular Kaizen is a popular alternative to standard or regular Kaizen. Despite its numerous similarities, the most significant difference between regular and Modular Kaizen is that the latter allows for employees to continue at their current workflow while working on implementation. Though its history shows that Modular Kaizen was originally used for manufacturing industries, it is now used in all industries. It is meant to increase business effectiveness and efficiency while improving processes and quality.

Benefits of Modular Kaizen

Perhaps the greatest benefit of implementing Modular Kaizen is the fact that regular work can proceed in the meantime. Other methods of process improvement are known to be time-consuming and bear a brunt of overhead costs. Some of these processes take employees away from their routine work for long periods of time, which has a negative effect on productivity. However, with Modular Kaizen that is not a concern, since the activities involved are dispersed and only require short sessions at a time. In many organizations, especially start-ups and small enterprises, it is not realistic to take away vital employees from their positions for the time frame required by regular Kaizen campaigns.

Another reason that Modular Kaizen is well accepted by organizations is that it ties in well with other methods of process improvement such as PDCA (Plan-Do-Check-Act) and DMAIC (Define-Measure-Analyze-Improve-Control). It is also a way to test team member's abilities to see if they are suited for handling more intrinsic methodologies of overall business process improvement.

Since Modular Kaizen looks at process, it is easier to pinpoint the origin of disruptions and to make the changes that are necessary to stop it from happening again. This lowers waste and unnecessary use of resources.

Employees that are involved in Modular Kaizen are given roles and responsibilities, which empower them so they feel valued and increase their morale. Such employees are more dedicated to their work and to the company thus. Modular Kaizen also requires a lot of collaboration; hence teamwork improves and has an indirect effect on people's judgment of situations outside of their department.

There are both short and long-term aspects to Modular Kaizen that are appealing. Goals are reached and problems are solved at an exceptional rate. Aside from that, regular monitoring and assessing of the processes (which take place after the implementation of Modular Kaizen) helps to bring about even greater improvement and flow of new ideas.

Limitations of Modular Kaizen

While there are many advantages of Modular Kaizen, which continue to bring success to the methodology, there are some limitations worth noting.

Modular Kaizen requires lots of preplanning and gathering of information to come up with a desirable plan of action. It is vital to understand and share the reasons for implementing Modular Kaizen for it to succeed in an organization. Also, it is important to encourage the idea that Modular

Kaizen is meant to be ongoing and to emphasize the longevity of the method.

It can be quite difficult to alter employee's understanding and attitude towards this entirely new concept. It is important to properly introduce all those involved in the reasoning behind Modular Kaizen methodology. Convincing employees that this method saves time, effort and money can be difficult since the benefits might not be seen immediately. Therefore, it is necessary to get those involved to think about the long-term effects instead of instant success. Consensus can take a while to reach and all members need to understand this to keep team morale up.

One of the limitations with introducing any type of novel management style is the buzz, which is often present at the beginning of the introduction tends to fizzle out after some time. This stops organizations from reaching the results they desired and can even deter organizations from choosing to follow-through in the correct way. This can cause employees to believe that the methodology was inefficient and to give up before the goal is reached.

It can be difficult to begin using Modular Kaizen, however proper introduction and understanding of the methodology can help make the process run better.

Unlike other methods, Modular Kaizen works on fixing the problem after it has occurred. This can be difficult for certain types of management, or certain organizations, to admit since it is clearly announcing that a problem occurred due to the fault of the business process. Some managers or operators may have a difficult time admitting to failure, which can hinder the development of a proper Modular Kaizen process.

Modular Kaizen is extremely beneficial in life sciences business process improvements dealing with- Audit findings, clinical trial studies, post-marketing surveillance (Phase IV) studies, control sample studies, stability studies, failure investigation, trend analysis, competitive benchmarking studies, logistics & supply chain routing studies, product returns, and destruction processes.

Flow Kaizen

Flow Kaizen (or Product Kaizen) deals with the flow of materials and information in an organization. It affects both revenues and organization culture.

Because it concerns materials, products, inventory, Flow Kaizen is usually effective within the warehouse, procurement, production, distribution and logistics areas of a life sciences company.

'Business transformation' or 'Turnaround campaigns' among others also involve Flow Kaizen. Traditionally, Flow Kaizen has been used in manufacturing-based industries. However, it is equally effective in service based organizations viz. retail, banks, call centers, airlines etc. or any business that includes a reasonable amount of customer service functions and processes.

Flow Kaizen shortens feedback cycles with short timescales.

The feedback tools may be 'pull-based' or 'push-based'; although pull-based feedback cycle is preferred. Examples of 'pull-based' cycles are-suggestion box, social media platforms, Kaizen cards (discussed in later chapters) or an informal coffee-time or water cooler conversation with employees about 'what is going on'. The 'push-based' feedback includes billboards, email notifications, newsletter and other one-way communications.

Process Kaizen

Process Kaizen improves employee work procedures, morale, and productivity. In Process Kaizen, the employees look for small wins i.e. ideas of small changes that can be implemented within the same day. Unlike other Kaizen types, Process

Kaizen doesn't have a lag time between 'concept' and 'implementation'.

Process Kaizen humanizes the workplace while eliminating Muri (Japanese term for hard work). It teaches employees to work efficiently and effectively to improve personal and departmental productivity. It also brings about better operations and total quality management within a company's products and services.

Tip: On a side note, automation also reduces hard work; however, it is not Process Kaizen. The reason being, automation fundamentally digresses from Kaizen principles.

The following equations explains Kaizen principle-

Kaizen = Respect for people.

Automation = Reducing workforce.

Therefore **Automation ≠ Kaizen**

Process Kaizen has objectives going beyond just productivity improvement. Process Kaizen focuses on eliminating Muri (i.e. overburden on the process, equipment, employee tasks).

Statistical experimental designs or Design of Experiments (DOE) used in research, product development, stability studies, scale-up, tech transfer, manufacturing site transfer campaigns, vendor approval studies are a scientific expression of Process Kaizen.

Process Kaizen mantra:

- Start where you are.
- Look for quick wins.
- Promote positive impact of procedural changes.
- Keep it small.

Tip: Kaizen methodology for organizational excellence essentially requires both Flow and Process Kaizen to be used judiciously.

People at all levels within a company- from CEO, managers, supervisors to the employee at the bottom of the corporate ladder must be equally involved in Process Kaizen for it to succeed; although the buck stops at the top!

Process Kaizen is a useful tool for Human Resources manager and department heads within the pharmaceutical, medical device and biotech industries to motivate and mobile workforce to meet corporate goals.

Agile Kaizen

Agile methodology helps define the project clearly with stakeholders, quick and effective project management with consistent and concise communication.

The Agile methodology uses the best process through empowered teams, customer involvement and the ability to analyze and control changes to the project scope at inception and throughout the lifecycle of the project. Combining Agile methodology with Kaizen results in reduced process steps, consistent and quick evolutionary improvements to projects, products, and services.

Agile Kaizen cuts process as well as project bottlenecks!

Agile Kaizen involves small increments always brought about by self-motivated, cross-functional teams that proceed and progress effortlessly. Agile Kaizen teams drive campaigns to eliminate root causes of most difficult problems within an organization.

Agile Kaizen works excellent with process improvements involving business strategy design and IT services within pharmaceutical, medical devices and biotech industries for example:

IS/IT departments, digital advertising, social media marketing, online and/or phone-based customer support, telemarketing, web-based businesses, online pharmacies, drug store management, supply chain logistics, ERP systems, inventory & warehouse management, electronic records management and all processes requiring 21 CFR Part 11 compliance.

Blitz Kaizen

Blitz Kaizen, otherwise known as 'Kaizen Event', involves any action that brings about a solution which improves current processes. It is a tool that is typically used in business process improvement by gathering important members of an organization into a single setting, mapping current processes through charts and diagrams, improving current processes and soliciting buy-in from those involved (whether directly or indirectly) in the process. Kaizen events offer a way to efficiently improve processes in a short amount of time.

Blitz Kaizen event is a weeklong activity, usually pre-planned to have a start and close date. The campaign comprises training sessions on the first day, process walking and its analysis on day-2, followed by two days of ideation to seek improvement solutions for the problem process. On the final day, everyone is trained on the 'new' process, a report is prepared and presented to the group prior to wrap-up.

Kaizen Blitz is meant to conduct events on a small scale that involve owners, managers, and operators to come up with improvement ideas that are deemed plausible by current participants in the process. Kaizen Blitz is short-term events that are meant to enhance a process by focusing on methods of improvement.

Implementing Kaizen Blitz typically causes the team members to participate in the event for an average of 5 days, meaning that they often cannot complete their regular work in the meantime. These events usually cover training, goal defining, brainstorming, designing, developing, implementing and documenting and are conducted by a team of important individuals in the organization.

These events typically take between two days to two weeks. It is possible for an organization to start noticing the benefits of Kaizen Blitz implementation just a week or two after its completion.

When Kaizen Blitz is implemented into the right situation it can truly help improve the organization. Employees that are part of Kaizen Blitz teams are often highly motivated and well-trained on Kaizen philosophies. It is necessary for Kaizen Blitz to be monitored and run by an individual who is highly skilled at dealing with people and who can conduct a good team. A powerful leader and team are vital to having success with Kaizen Blitz.

Kaizen Blitz implementation involves several stages. To begin with, the problem must be defined. Data that explains the current processes is then recorded. The ideal goal for the problem is visualized, which makes it easier to come up with the various stages that are involved in reaching the goal. The team is then responsible for creating new ideas by brainstorming options to deal with the problem.

This is when the Kaizen plan is developed. Once the plan is completed, it is then implemented. Through the implementation, data is recorded and measured continuously to make comparisons between results. After comparisons are made, documents are created that summarize the events that took place during Kaizen Blitz and its findings. An action plan is later created to make the solution adjustable to similar circumstances, or to be used later.

Benefits of Kaizen Blitz

One of the best advantages of using Kaizen Blitz is that it works on a specific goal. There are times when coming up with a new goal gets drawn out or pushed under the table. However, with Kaizen Blitz that is not an option. Results are required urgently and with great attention to detail. It encourages people to come up with solutions instead of excuses.

Kaizen Blitz results are substantial and easy to notice. This is great for boosting employee morale since it makes people feel enthusiastic. It is also a great way to introduce Six Sigma and/or other methods such as Lean Manufacturing to a company that has no experience with these methodologies. Kaizen Blitz introduces improvement ideas to employees in a way that is not threatening and allows people to see rapid results. There are many other advantages that come from implementing Kaizen Blitz.

The results are fast and the solutions are obvious. The goals of Kaizen Blitz are achievable by following actions which make it easier for involvement from other members of the organization and therefore improves communication within the workforce. It also lowers waste, cost, and resources while bringing about quicker and better results, profitability and productivity.

Since Kaizen Blitz requires actions to reach a goal, it must have achievable stages or milestones. These stages require individuals to contribute their time to fulfilling the requirements of each stage. The quickest Kaizen Blitz campaign can take one or two days and the results are noticeable in a week or two.

Tip: While it is a great tool for certain circumstances, Kaizen Blitz is not intended as a replacement for other change management methodologies.

Limitations of Kaizen Blitz

Training is an important factor during Kaizen Blitz, but it is often seen as a superficial act and not intensive enough. Blitz events take place over a short period, it is not enough for those involved to truly understand many of the aspects relating to the Kaizen Blitz methodology and its principles.

Kaizen Blitz pays significant attention to detail and works on specific areas of an organization to solve problems and/or improve processes. While it may be good for the specific area, this can have a detrimental effect on the process. It can also be difficult to anticipate how the solutions to one problem will affect everything else. This can be tackled by making sure that teams are made up of various representatives, information is shared across departments and more importantly, events are planned strategically after considering its overall impact on the company.

After Kaizen Blitz is completed it is typical for the organization to forget about continuing with the changes. Therefore, it is necessary to maintain and monitor the results after the Blitz campaign is over. Other times, management commitment is lacking and hinders the changes from being implemented.

Kaizen Blitz may be applied for process improvement to all departments within the pharmaceutical, medical device, and biotech industries.

Tip: Kaizen Blitz offers practical solutions to reducing costs in an organization. Since the ideas presented are often small and practical, they also often don't require any investment.

Daily Kaizen

Daily Kaizen as the name implies, are continuous improvement activities practiced daily. It is practiced not just by designated Kaizen teams, but by all employees within the organization.

Daily Kaizen practices the following 'daily' routines:

- Monitor standards.

- Find potential upgrades to standard.

- Create systems and procedures to solve problems quickly.

- Solve problems quickly to keep performance to standard.

- Raise the standard bar consistently.

- Review performances weekly or frequently to keep employees engaged and enhance their creativity.

- Create and sustain a culture of 'Continuous Improvement' within the company.

Advantages of Daily Kaizen

- Ensures alignment of employee taskforce with corporate objectives.

- Improves communication, transparency and motivation within the company.

- Creates new 'standards' and increases team productivity.

- Minimizes 'deviations' and impact thereof.

Daily Kaizen can be applied to all departments within the pharmaceutical, medical device and biotech industries; especially to Project Management activities. Daily Kaizen ensures projects are run on time-scope-budget schedule.

A brief pause ...

Various types of Kaizen give customized solutions to a variety of business problems. The best benefit is obtained by combining Lean Kaizen with one or more Kaizen type(s). In addition, combining Lean Kaizen with Just-in-time, Jidoka, Kanban and/or Total Productive Maintenance (TPM) methodology gives incredible results.

Tip: Remember: Not all problems require a Kaizen event to resolve them. A company must always have a bunch of 4 to 5 different process

83

improvement methodologies in their tool kit. You might want to check out my book entitled, 'Business Process Improvement for Manufacturing and Service Industry' which presents 18 different time-tested process improvement techniques.

Tip: There must be a documented SOP for choosing business process improvement methodology for your organization. The idea is to avoid a *right method* being used to solve a *wrong problem*. You might want to check out my book entitled, 'How to choose business process methodology for your organization and measure the positive change' which presents practical ways to choose business process methodology for improving processes and to make exponential increase in profits.

A major factor impacting business efficiency is process waste. In-control processes eliminate or the least minimize waste and ring-in huge savings.

The key question here is- How to identify waste and 'hidden' inefficiencies that take a toll on your organization's revenues?

We will address this in the next chapter ...

Chapter 3: Identifying inefficiencies?

In this chapter, we will see ...

- ✓ What comprises Business Inefficiency?

- ✓ Different types of Waste.

- ✓ How to identify Workplace Inefficiency?

- ✓ List of 'Hidden' inefficiencies that take toll on your organization's revenue.

Shruti Bhat

What has Kaizen to offer the highly regulated pharmaceutical, medical devices and biotech industry?

The answer is simple, yet profound. Kaizen helps identify inefficiencies at your workplace and/or the entire business, and takes your business from being Good to Great!

Also, Kaizen helps you stay ahead of your competition. How?

- Kaizen can be practiced in startups as well as large companies. Kaizen identifies inefficiencies and eliminates or minimizes waste.

- Kaizen creates value, not just in the product, but also in the business's very existence- its governance, functioning, finance, clientele, sustenance, and growth.

This value creation increases top line and market share. The waste control further augments bottom line; all of this is achieved with minimal investments, isn't that awesome?

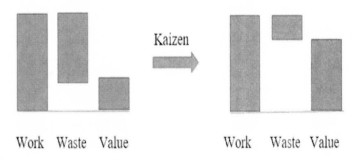

87

In this chapter, I shall elaborate on value-creation using Kaizen and discuss potential business inefficiencies, waste, waste control or elimination techniques.

What comprises Business inefficiency?

Business aka workplace is a system, which happens when business people interact with customers using a business process. Therefore, anything that removes inefficiencies in this system automatically helps improve business's bottom line.

The business process is a sequence of events necessary to design, produce and distribute products and/or services. Workplace/ business system comprises of its premises, people, and processes; these 3Ps ultimately govern products and profits!

To identify and understand business inefficiency, let us briefly touch upon few terms-

- **Process Time**- Time from Start to Finish. It is the sum of both value-adding and wasteful activities/ time.

- **VA (Value-Added) Activity**- All activities that convert raw material to finished goods, which is what the customer pays for.

- **NV (Non-Value-Added) Activity**- These are activities that consume costs and add no value to the product (or service).

However, some activities such as inspection, product approval wait times, income tax returns filing and the like are few examples of non-value-added activities. But these are critical for a business's survival and growth. Hence, despite being non-value-added items strictly in terms of definition, they are not optional. Excluding such activities, all non-value-added items are called 'waste' or 'Muda' (in Japanese).

There are 8 to 10 types of waste. Mathematically, 'value' and 'muda' are proportional to each other; as 'waste' decreases, 'value' increases.

Value = Value added activities + (- Waste)

Here is the crux of the challenge-increasing 'value' is therefore not just increasing the proportion of 'value-added' activities in a business, it also means one needs to cut down 'waste'.

The 'value' can't increase unless there is a paradigm shift in the way pharmaceutical, device or the entire life sciences sector runs its business (process).

Sadly, in most pharmaceutical, medical device and biotech companies, process improvement activities happen only with 'technical' processes such as- research, product formulation, testing, and manufacturing. Business process improvement doesn't happen at all or is met with extreme resistance. Often, the 'regulations' are cited as 'shield' or excuse to prevent business process changes, improvements or re-design.

In other instances, decision makers and professionals who know the regulatory aspects are not made aware of benefits of business process changes. They are blissfully unaware of how Lean Six Sigma or Kaizen might be integrated into the value-stream of their highly-regulated business. And as is said- you don't know what you don't know, so status-quo remains...

"The challenge today is not about bringing forth business process changes within a pharmaceutical company. The real challenge is how to bring on this paradigm shift within the industry vertical at large, and make Kaizen or any appropriate business process improvement technique, an integral part of the company's operations and governance." – Dr. Shruti U. Bhat

Here is a picture of published statistics of how Man, Machine, and Materials spend time in a factory-

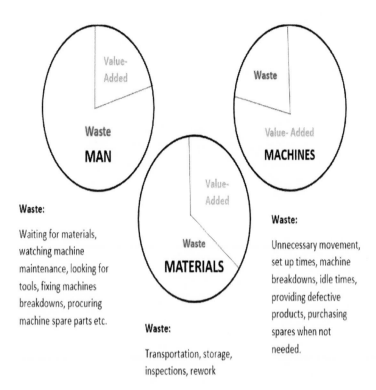

Pharmaceutical, medical device or biotech factory is not very different...

Reducing throughput time reduces the inventory, meaning- less working capital, quicker deliveries, greater financial flexibility and increased productivity. Accelerated ROI is the name of the game and this game can't be won unless one understands it from end-to-end i.e. the value-stream and identify waste as well as the 'hidden' inefficiencies that take a toll on the company's revenues.

Different types of waste

Here's a quick comparison of commonly found wastes in manufacturing and office premises-

Muda in Manufacturing	Muda in Office
Sending out defective products	Passing on work containing errors
Waiting for inspection, test reports	Waiting for signature approvals, bureaucracy
Walking, transporting materials	Walking, re-routing documents back-n-forth
Over production, Over processing	Too many print outs, copies, emails, files, lots of paper and electronic data
Excess inventory, quarantine and WIP	Excess documentation

Typically, waste can be classified as-

Type 1 Waste (Muda): Actions that are non-value added but are for some other reason deemed necessary. Example- regulatory demands, approval wait times, facility and/or machine maintenance downtime, waiting for test results, accounting requirements etc. therefore cannot be eliminated easily.

Type 2 Waste (Muda): Non-value-added and unnecessary; these should be the first target for removal.

Together these Types 1 and 2 wastes form what I call 'The Kaizen Muda Chakra'.

Tip: Chakra is a wheel and it signifies 'motion'. The 'Kaizen Muda Chakra' proposes that, eliminating these eight mudas, will gear your business in 'motion' such as, from being Good to Great!

When activities that drive-up cycle times and/or cost are eliminated, processes become effective and profitable.

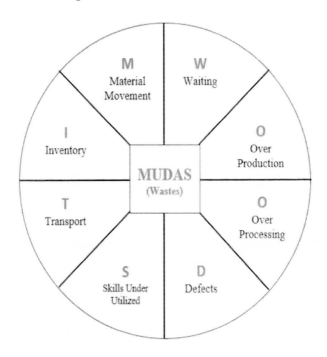

The Kaizen Muda Chakra

Below are nine areas to investigate using Kaizen, for commonly found wastes that consume unnecessary dollars, and time.

Over Production: *Producing more than demand*

Operations, when run along 'pull' system, brings better ROI. The 'pull' system, a Lean Kaizen terminology simply means, start manufacture only when there is a pull exerted by customer demand and manufacture quantities as per the 'pull'. The pull system of production, therefore, keeps work-in-progress (WIP) and inventories low.

A point to note is what causes over-production? Usually, it is attributed to poor line balancing, capacities not matching production demands, machines run at different speeds giving varied throughput.

Besides 'pull' system, another alternative is to go for Design for Manufacture (DFM), Continuous Manufacturing, 3D Printing and Synchronized Manufacturing which includes-demand driven production, the logical rhythm of production through the supply chain and moving via downstream signals.

Take-a-Five

Take five minutes to think and jot down answers to the following questions-

- Is 'Over-Production' waste present in your organization?
- Does this waste affect you adversely in your line of work? If yes, to what extent?
- Which workplaces do you think this waste affects most in your organization?

Tip: A pull system is where processes are based on customer demand. The concept is that each process manufactures every component in-line with another department to build a final product matching design and delivery needs of the customer. Since goods are produced as per customer demand, only what is deliverable gets manufactured.

Inventory: *Storing more materials than necessary.*

Just like over-production, storing more materials than necessary is a waste.

Inventory waste could arise from buying excess raw materials, or unused materials lying in the warehouse, long manufacturing or testing processes resulting in large quantities of quarantined goods, logistics methods not up-to-date, near expiry goods lying in the distribution channel etc.

Minimizing inventory frees up huge capital investment, resources and maintains a healthy cash flow. Just-in-time, FIFO (First in First out), centralized warehousing and Kanban are proven beneficial tools in eliminating 'Inventory' waste.

Take-a-Five

Take five minutes to think and jot down answers to the following questions-

- Is 'Inventory' type waste present in your organization?
- Does this waste affect you adversely in your line of work? If yes, to what extent?
- Which workplaces do you think this waste affects most in your organization?

Transportation: *Unnecessary movement of materials.*

cGMP compliance and safety regulations usually propel pharmaceutical, medical device and biotech companies to build complex rooms for people flow, lots of changeover benches, doors, rooms within rooms with one door leading into another one.

Also, too many conveyors or hatches for material flow. Although cGMP compliance is the baseline need, pharmaceutical companies tend to design facilities only with regards to cGMP regulations.

A vital aspect of facility design is to keep it 'Lean', prevent 'Waste' and facilitate 'Production' while still complying with cGMP norms. Design for Manufacture (DFM) prevents *transportation waste* and hence must be used while creating new production sites.

DFM creates facilities after considering internal logistics, as well as flow issues. DFM integrates flow management into the cGMP fabric to create state-of-the-art production room layouts.

But, what about facilities already existing and operational? Site modification within pharmaceutical, medical device, and biotech business is a big change, requiring re-submission of product dossiers, regulatory approvals before products could be produced or sold. Site modification, therefore, hits both belt (pun intended) and the wallet!

So, how can we minimize or eliminate transportation waste from facilities already existing and operational? Lean Kaizen helps in such cases.

Lean Kaizen can be fully integrated into cGMP framework of an existing facility, without the hassles and expenses of re-submissions and/or product re-approvals!

Up to 45% transportation waste elimination is quite easily achieved by practicing Lean Kaizen; which means a huge percentage of overhead expenses are directly saved, isn't it awesome?

Take-a-Five

Take five minutes to think and jot down answers to the following questions-

- Is 'Transportation' type of waste present in your organization?
- Does this waste affect you adversely in your line of work? If yes, to what extent?
- Which workplaces do you think this waste affects most in your organization?

Waiting: *Any kind of delay is classified as 'waiting' type of waste.*

Delays occur from various quarters. Few examples are- scientists wait for materials to be sourced by procurement department, who in turn wait for accounts department to release payments; formulation experts wait to get results from testing labs.

Production operators wait to receive batch cards from quality department, or to get material dispensed by warehouse, or for machines to get set up by maintenance folks; products wait to get packed or to get 'approved and released' by quality control or wait because of a shift change or product changeover.

Waiting, because of bureaucracy prevalent in organizational culture; departments not working at full productivity because they are waiting for Human Resources to bring on new recruits.

Business development team waiting for expansion plans or go/no-go decisions from senior management; employees wait for 'bosses' approval, the list is endless. Do these instances seem too familiar?

Usually, up to 20% of employee time is spent daily in 'Waiting' resulting in lost productivity!

Take-a-Five

Take five minutes to think and jot down answers to the following questions-

- Is 'Waiting' type of waste present in your organization?
- Does this waste affect you adversely in your line of work? If yes, to what extent?

- Which workplaces do you think this waste affects most in your organization?

Over-Processing: *More than necessary process steps.*

Outdated process, poor tooling, poor facility design and/or improper product design & development contribute to 'Over Processing' type of waste.

Another type of 'Over-Processing' is employees working after office hours. In some offices, working late is recognized as being 'loyal and hard working' and rewarded. Instead, what it must mean is that employees are either task overloaded or acting busy to disguise their inefficiency.

Rewarding inefficient employees will de-motivate and/or demoralize true performers. Such employees will soon look for other pastures. Overloaded employees will soon feel the burnout and look for opportunities elsewhere. High employee turnover rate is a direct by-product of 'Over-processing' type of waste.

Take-a-Five

Take five minutes to think and jot down answers to the following questions-

- Is 'Over-Processing' type of waste present in your organization?
- Does this waste affect you adversely in your line of work? If yes, to what extent?
- Which workplaces do you think this waste affects most in your organization?

Wasted Motion: *Unnecessary movement of people reaching out for files, spares, tools, printouts, information etc.*

This is more prevalent in open offices and wide hall type of production areas. Such workplaces were designed with an aim to improve capacities, bring-forth team spirit among employees, a landscape to share and bond with your colleagues.

Visualize- a common printer among a group of 5-10 employees. Each time a printout is needed, the employee must move towards the printer to get it. They meet others on their way and get into idle chit-chatting. Nothing wrong with that, it is human nature and creates mini-bonds between employees (the very reason why open offices evolved).

The lop side is, a lot of time gets wasted due to such unnecessary movements, employees get distracted, lose focus with their tasks resulting in lowered productivity.

Take-a-Five

Take five minutes to think and jot down answers for the following questions-

- Is 'Wasted Motion' type of waste present in your organization?
- Does this waste affect you adversely in your line of work? If yes, to what extent?
- Which workplaces do you think this waste affects most in your organization?

Re-Work: *Anything not done right first time and is being redone.*

Re-Work in pharmaceutical, medical device and biotech manufacturing is not appreciated. In cases where product dossiers are registered with USFDA and other strict regulators, the scope of re-work is nearly impossible. Companies dealing in markets of third-world countries and emerging economies, however, do tend to practice re-work with batch carry-over up to 25%.

Re-work happens in non-production areas as well. Too many photostat copies or document printouts, frequent machine breakdowns, extraordinary numbers of work orders to maintenance division, rising number of purchase orders to procurement departments, too many experiments conducted by formulation scientists, an extraordinary number of repeat analysis done by testing labs are few examples.

Another major form of re-work deals with document creation. For example- bill of materials, manufacturing batch cards, standard operating procedures (SOP), test procedures, raw material and finished product specifications, process optimization protocols etc. Tons of paper and man-hours are spent in pharmaceutical R&Ds at the time of each new product scale-up.

Re-work is infamously addressed as 'hidden factory'. It is often said that mistakes provide great learning opportunities. This isn't always true, especially when there are better options available for not to make mistakes, by utilizing Poka-Yoke or mistake proofing!

Take-a-Five

Take five minutes to think and jot down answers to the following questions-

- Is 'Re-Work' type of waste present in your organization?
- Does this waste affect you adversely in your line of work? If yes, to what extent?
- Which workplaces do you think this waste affects most in your organization?

Un-Utilized Resources: *Under or un-utilized talent and skills of employees.*

How many times have you noticed formulation scientists sitting in front of a computer for hours typing out batch cards or HPLC analyst typing test procedures? Typing must be left to data-entry operators? With appropriate training, these data-entry operators do wonderful jobs.

Ideally, the formulation scientist should be developing formulations themselves or coaching others. The HPLC expert should be busy developing cost-effective test procedures and ensuring accurate results are provided quickly to development scientists. Together, the formulation scientist and HPLC expert, must think of ways of shortening product development timelines!

Take-a-Five

Take five minutes to think and jot down answers to the following questions-

- Is 'Un-utilized Resources' type of waste present in your organization?
- Does this waste affect you adversely in your line of work? If yes, to what extent?
- Which workplaces do you think this waste affects most in your organization?

Defects: *Includes scrap, errors, and product rejects etc.*

If a non-compliant batch is not re-worked, then it must be scrapped using eco-friendly destruction procedures. Likewise, with time-expired finished goods, returns and in-process material reject. Destruction procedures in life sciences companies are elaborate and must comply with cGMP and local city regulations. Very often, companies outsource this activity.

This is a dual loss- it costs money to first produce and then to destroy!

Take-a-Five

Take five minutes to think and jot down answers to the following questions-

- Is 'Defect' type of waste present in your organization?

- Does this waste affect you adversely in your line of work? If yes, to what extent?
- Which workplaces do you think this waste affects most in your organization?

  Tip: A compilation of your above answers will give a preliminary list of wastes prevalent in your organization.

Take five minutes to think and complete this short exercise.

- Which types of wastes are present at your workplace?
- Create a Process Waste Scorecard: Divide your organization or department into different zones.
  Identify and jot down different types of wastes you find in processes worked in each zone.
  Assign a score on a scale 0-4 (0: no waste found; 1: very little waste; 2: low waste; 3: considerable waste; 4: a lot of waste).
  Sum up the scores for each waste per process and record final score.

Process Waste Card:

Process Name	Department	9 Types of wastes									✿	Final Score
		Over Production	Inventory	Transportation	Waiting	Over Processing	Wasted Motion	Rework	Un-utilized resources	Defects		

*Based on your results from Take-a-Five exercise, add columns as necessary to the above process waste card. Note- attach data such as interview/ survey/ photos, observations from other short Kaizen events, suggestions received etc. Prepare a summary report to help identify the business process problem.

Also, take few more minutes to note down answers to following questions-

- What causes the wastes identified in your Process Waste Scorecard? Can you think of ideas to eliminate them?
- What operations and/or business process are you responsible for in your company?
- What do you do that is value-added?
- What do you think you can do to minimize or eliminate waste?
- What do you think can be done by your colleagues to reduce waste?

Save and park your answers, we will re-visit them later.

So far, we have discussed what could be termed as known mudas /wastes. The crux of the challenge lies in identifying the 'hidden' mudas i.e. inefficiencies.

These 'hidden' inefficiencies resemble the leak in a pot which can never get filled-up, no matter what the effort or investment. How to identify 'hidden' inefficiencies that take a toll on your organization's revenues?

Let us explore...

How to identify 'hidden' inefficiencies and wastes that take a toll on your organization's revenues?

"If you do not know what your problem is, all solutions are bad"

- Unknown

To identify inefficiencies hidden or otherwise, one needs to understand the current process, also termed Workflow or Flow. A commonly used tool to depict workflow is Process Mapping.

Process Mapping

Process mapping is a tool used to show workflow in a visual manner. It is also used as an organizational tool for communicating ideas and planning within businesses.

Business processes briefly describe the chain of events that are involved in an activity or a group of activities. It is common to use a business process if the activities influence current products or data and bring about production. Few examples include invoicing, product shipping details, updating information, tracking orders and allocating budgets. Business processes mapping can be done at any level throughout an organization.

The main aspects of process mapping include- inputs, outputs, stages, decision points, and functions. The information that is made available through process mapping allows those who view it to gain insight into steps, which are paired with brief explanations.

The diagram that represents a business process is typically known as a notation. Various computer software makes it possible to create business processes electronically, however simple business processes are just as effective when written with pen and paper. Some find it better to jot down the processes on a piece of paper, or on several small ones, to kick start their creativity and thinking process.

The reason for process mapping is to have a greater understanding. The way these process maps are displayed makes it easier for viewers to ask the right questions and to give appropriate suggestions for improvement. Further, the visual representation style of process map makes it easier to understand complex details without having to read an excessive amount of text, saving a lot of time. Process maps can be considered as scientific micro-Learning.

Process mapping also makes it easier to see where there are faults or unnecessary stages in a process.

Tip: It is necessary to evaluate and have members of the project confirm the accuracy of the process map after the map is created. This will help save time and effort from making changes further down the line.

How to map business process?

The prerequisite to mapping a successful business process is to understand the reason for using the tool. To create a map of current processes, it is necessary to come up with both a 'Discovery map' and a 'Process diagram'.

Discovery map is the initial stage of developing a business process map since it defines the capacity, identifies members and describes the goals for improvement. The basics that are required from a discovery map include-information, involvement, guides and communication. It is common for employee teams to come up with the discovery map. Teams should be small and must include a project leader, facilitator, and sponsor.

Process diagram uses the information from a discovery map and adds planning to the ideas. The goal of creating a process diagram is to add detail and organization to the ideas presented during the development of the discovery map.

Based on results of value stream mapping, a company's senior management decides the process to be improved. Alternately, employees could come up with process change ideas. After the target process for improvement has been chosen, a map is developed. Maps use between six to ten boxes to show the main stages in a process. When creating the map, two key ideas are kept in mind, namely-effective communication and the main problems.

The map works as a great tool for effective communication since it allows everyone to have enough information about all stages in the process. It also helps them to see what or who is not involved. The main problems should be identified early-on during the creation of the map, which makes it easier for analysis and evaluation later.

The main ideas that the facilitator should keep in mind include: knowing the beginning and final stages, process naming, and activities included in each stage and documentation. The facilitator has several responsibilities such as- to keep track of the entire process and to make an analysis of the effectiveness of the map later.

The business processes within organizations globally, across all industry sectors including pharmaceutical, medical device, and biotech companies follow Pareto's rule.

Pareto's 80/20 rule, otherwise known as the Pareto principle, is the idea that 80 percent of the results arise from 20 percent of total problems. The main focal point of Pareto's 80/20 rule for an organization is to remember that focusing on the important 20 percent is crucial to the success of the organization.

It implies that 20 percent of daily activities are what truly counts since they cause the 80 percent of results. Thus, one needs to focus on the right 20 percent problems to maximize impacts. This requires evaluation on what matters should make up the 20 percent, which will help keep the focus on the essential activities.

There are several stages when it comes to implementing Pareto's 80/20 rule. These include: identifying the problems, identifying the root-cause of the various problems, grouping problems by their root-cause, scoring the groups and implementing a plan of action. The group with the highest score should be a top priority; while the group with the lowest score should be last. It is up to the organization to decide whether a software or traditional method will work best for this task.

Business processes are known to work best when there is input, support, and ideas from various people that are involved in the organization (or department).

Identifying inefficiencies:

- Measurements/ Brainstorming sessions with employees.

- Customer complaints (VOC- Voice of the customer).

- Talk to vendors.

- Internal communications.

Identifying the best way to detect inefficiencies: Gemba- 'Going to where work happens' choosing the right business process improvement methodology which in turn depends on the company- its size, goals, and culture.

Pointers to inefficiencies

Productivity: lead times, throughput time or takt time, time to market, process capability, floor space utilization, labor cost, sales returns, defect rate, training.

Customer levels: Market share, the number of new customers, repeat customers, customer response time.

Finances: NPV, inventory turns, expenses per department, budgets Vs actual cost, the number of shipments, market penetration.

Discovering 'hidden' waste from process maps via 5 steps-

1. Look at the three core areas i.e. Facility, Facts and WIP.

2. Ask What? Find answers to what is the operation or process all about.

3. Ask Why? Find answers to why is this operation or process necessary.

4. List all items that are necessary for operation or process. Any step that is essential to execute the operation/ process is 'work'. Anything that is not work is 'waste or inefficiency'.

5. Use 5-Whys technique to each identified waste identified in steps 1-4, to lead to the real or 'hidden' inefficiency.

Take-a-Five

Take five minutes to think and jot down answers to the following questions-

- What are five different types of wastes happening in operations/process you work with or are responsible for?
- Does this waste affect your operational productivity or deliverability?
- Note down one improvement idea for each waste you have identified.

List of 'Hidden' inefficiencies that take toll on your organization's revenue

Typically, the 'hidden' inefficiencies in a pharmaceutical company reside in following twenty-five key business processes-

i. Main product technology in business/ operation process.

ii. Housekeeping and building maintenance.

iii. Team collaboration and conflict management.

iv. Organogram: Strategic rationalizing and integration of different departments within an organization.

v. Quality assurance system, zero defect identification tools, quality policy.

vi. Outsourcing partners/ suppliers/ vendor management.

vii. Production/ workplace facility design and EHS compliance.

viii. Product distribution logistics and delivery.

ix. The feedback loop of customer comments.

x. Value chain & Customer conversion rate.

xi. Machinery design & automation.

xii. Reducing machinery downtime (cleaning, breakdowns, spares, setups, changeovers, idling) and manufacturing scheduling.

xiii. Minimizing/ eliminating reworks, work in process (WIP), quarantine goods.

xiv. Minimizing/ eliminating product returns.

xv. Product/ company marketing and brand building.

xvi. Economic order quantities (EOQ), material procurement procedures, inventory management.

xvii. Batch and Continuous production process.

xviii. Human resource training and continuous development.

xix. The financial health of the business, cash flow, and its tenacity.

xx.   The fluidity of the enterprise to adapt to the dynamic business environment and offer a competitive advantage.

xxi. Time management practices.

xxii. Controlling utilities and overheads.

xxiii. Information technology/ ERP systems.

xxiv. Employee recruitment, empowerment, retention, and training.

xxv. Innovation, product development, knowledge management, and intellectual property management.

The questions to ask ourselves are:

- What are we doing to reduce these waste/ inefficiencies?

- How much of this waste/ inefficiency can be eliminated?

- How much of our time is spent on eliminating waste/ inefficiencies at work?

- Do we know how much dollar savings can be achieved through Continuous Improvement efforts?

Tip: Organizations usually take short cuts to become efficient by introducing process automation. A common question around process automation is- How do I eliminate human errors by passing it on to a machine? However, automation must be done after careful thinking, viz. study which tasks should I never entrust to a machine? Knowing when to tip toe and when to leap, or run both systems side-by-side.

Take-a-Five

Take a step back and review the negative impact inefficiencies in all forms are having on you/ your workplace right now! After review, come up with a strategy and do a cost- benefit analysis i.e. a comparative assessment of all costs to introduce the improvement solutions, perform it and support changes resulting from all benefits you expect from it. Also, do the costing for opportunity loss i.e. cost of running the process as-is.

Park your answers, we will revisit them later.

Tip: In case you wish to discuss your answers with me, please contact me at http://www.drshrutibhat.com with your query. I take one hour FREE Continuous Improvement Workshop each month via WebEx, to interact with my readers.

Process inefficiencies cost 20- 30% of revenues to businesses each year! Imagine what your company could do if it had 20% extra funds?

What are the tools to identify Process wastes? We will address this in the next chapter ...

Chapter 4: Kaizen tools

In this chapter, we will see ...

- ✓ Root Cause Analysis

- ✓ Check Sheets

- ✓ Control Charts

- ✓ Pareto Charts

- ✓ Histogram

- ✓ Run Charts

- ✓ Scatter Diagram

- ✓ Kaizen Idea Collection tools

- ✓ Affinity Diagrams

- ✓ Tree Diagrams

- ✓ FMEA

- ✓ CPM & PERT

- ✓ PDPC

- ✓ Arrow Diagram

- ✓ Kamishibai Boards

- ✓ 5W+1H

- ✓ Value Stream Mapping

- ✓ Thought leader insights

Kaizen process improvement methodology employs several types of tools, such as-

✓ Tools to identify process inefficiencies.

✓ Tools to collect ideas for designing Kaizen strategies.

✓ Tools to implement Kaizen campaigns.

✓ Tools to manage Kaizen projects.

✓ Tools to track Kaizen success.

✓ Tools to sustain Kaizen culture.

As many as 150 different tools are available for use. Each of these tools has alternative options, advantages, and limitations. The choice of tool depends on the process inefficiency, organizational culture, project budget and personal preference of the Kaizen leader.

This book mentions some of the commonly employed tools during successful Kaizen campaigns.

Let us consider them one by one...

Root Cause Analysis Diagram

Root Cause Analysis Diagram alternately known as Cause-and-Effect (C&E) diagram, Fishbone or Ishikawa diagram, depict the causes of individual events and the connection between the events. They detect problems and facilitate potential process changes. C&E diagrams are used to pinpoint the cause of a specific process problem as they make it easier to identify the problem to fix the issue.

Root cause analysis requires the collection of data, identification of the root cause, charting of information regarding the cause and suggestions for making changes and implementing them. There are different methods for conducting root cause analysis which can be applied to different circumstances.

There are three vital steps to perform a root cause analysis. The steps include defining the problem and its effect on goals, analyzing the root causes through visual representation via mapping and preventing unsatisfactory impacts by choosing the solutions that are effective. During 'Defining stage' one asks- "What is the problem?" During 'Analyzing stage' one asks- "Why did it happen?". While, at stage three that is "Preventing stage', one asks- "What will be done?"

A root cause map is constructed during a root cause analysis in order to determine the reason for an incident's occurrence in a visual manner. It links the various relationships to come up with potential causes. The relationships that are considered are cause and effect types. It is meant to be a simple map; however, some situations require much more detailed maps.

A root cause map begins on the right-hand side by stating the problem. The map then involves arrows that point viewers into the direction of causes by asking 'Why' each time. Every time "Why" is asked, the response is added to the right of the respective boxes. The questions continue five times until the root cause of the problem is clearly identifiable. The "Why" questioning leads to answers which easily detect when the optimal state of the process has been sacrificed or altered.

Brainstorming is yet another technique of conducting root cause analysis. Brainstorming is also used to come up with solutions once the cause has been determined. Once the analysis is complete, the information is shared for others to understand the root cause of an issue.

Check Sheet

Check Sheet is a tool that allows for the collection of information regarding quality issues. Check sheets for quality problems scores a number of problems for several predetermined defect causes. Once the check sheet is complete, the total score of problems for individual causes can then be used to make a Pareto chart or a histogram.

Histograms

Histograms are used to give a rough assessment of the probability of a source of a problem. It shows the occurrences of observations that occur amongst the subject focus point.

Pareto Charts

Pareto Charts contain line graph and bars to graph data. It is a method of finding out where the sources for defects come from and pinpointing the source of the largest reoccurring defect. Pareto charts are easy to understand due to its simple detailed visual presentation.

Run Charts

Run Charts and stratification, depict the stages involved in a process. They allow viewers to easily identify and solve issues of quality problems by clearly showing the details of a certain procedure.

Control Charts

Control Charts are made up of a horizontal line that represents the norm of the process. There is also a line above and below, to represent upper and lower regulation boundaries. Various samples are gathered over a time period and added to the chart. If measurements are found to extend above or below the regulation boundary lines, indicates a quality problem exists and must be investigated.

Scatter Diagrams

Scatter diagrams depict the connection between variables. By comparing two variables, it is easy to see where there is a correlation or where one is lacking.

Kaizen idea collection tools

Kaizen idea collection tools include Kaizen cards (discussed in later chapters), web-based applications called Kaizen tracker which helps in idea collection, designing strategies as well as the implementation of Kaizen suggestions, alternately called Kaizen Initiatives (KI).

It records number of KI submitted annually, department wise and computes the percentage of KI led changes in departments each year. It highlights names and numbers of employees submitting at least one KI per year, overall employee participation in the campaign and percentage participation by employee(s) year on year. It also serves as Kaizen campaign performance metric.

Affinity Diagram

Affinity Diagram is used to organize ideas and data stemming after a brainstorming or mind mapping session. It helps re-group the information based on their affinity or natural relationship for data review and analysis, survey response and voice of customer studies, contextual inquiries for

123

interview feedback analysis etc. It streamlines ideas using three simple steps-

1. Record each idea on an index card or sticky note.
2. Regroup ideas that are similar in topic, context, and data or seem to be related. Subgroup large clusters as needed.
3. Sort out each card until all cards have been exhausted.

The success of Affinity diagram is based on recording all ideas as they come. Ideas collected from a cross-functional team and all stakeholders within an organization are more useful.

Regrouping and identifying relationship must be done as next step to produce accurate Affinity diagrams. They may be further used to create C&E diagrams.

Tree Diagrams

Tree Diagram or decision trees are very common in pharmaceutical/ medical device realm and are created based on its intended use and performance.

Typically expressed as CT(X) trees- CTQ- Critical to quality, CTD- Critical to delivery, CTS- Critical to safety, CTP- Critical to process, CTC- Critical to cost, CTF- Critical to the facility, CTM- Critical to manufacturing.

FMEA

FMEA failure mode and effects analysis tools help in identifying risks modes, consequences of failure and mitigation plans.

There are two types of risks- Inherent risk which is a risk that existed in the absence of any action or control or modification of the event and Residual risk, a risk that remains after controls are implemented.

The risk is the potential of losing something of value, weighed against the potential to gain something of value. Risk hinders the achievement of objectives and it has two attributes:

1. Likelihood: Probability of risk event

2. Consequence: Impact of risk event

FMEA creates prioritized risk levels through rating relative risks for each potential failure mode.

CPM & PERT Program management tools:

Critical path method (CPM) is used for projects that assure deterministic activity times i.e. the times at which each activity will be carried out are known.

Programs Evaluation and Review Technique (PERT) on the other hand, allows for stochastic activity times; the times at which each activity will be carried out are uncertain or varied.

Because of this core difference, CPM and PERT are used in different contexts. Regardless of the methodology employed careful considerations must be given to the overall project objectives, timelines, cost as well as the roles & responsibilities of all participants & stakeholders.

RACI

RACI Matrix defines the contributions from different roles when it comes to finishing tasks in a business process. It is a beneficial tool for making sure that roles and role responsibilities are clearly understood in a process.

RACI matrix provides a good tool for eliminating confusion and allowing those involved to fulfill their roles in a more timely and effective manner, which leads to project completion at a more desirable rate. A RACI matrix is commonly made by creating rows and columns that depict the processes and the roles relating to those processes.

RACI is an acronym for Responsible, Accountable, Consulted and Informed.

Responsible refers to the individual that is executing the activity. Accountable refers to the person who makes authority decisions and approves work. Consult refers to the individuals that are consulted when activities or decisions are being made or analyzed. Inform refers to the group of people who must be updated on the actions or decisions in a process.

A RACI matrix is advantageous to an organization because it clearly shows if there are not enough, or too many, responsibilities in relation to each role. It also allows those involved to be aware of the responsibilities and the accountability of each activity. It makes it easier to inform all the right people and often allows for better communication to take place instead of misunderstandings. It also saves a significant amount of time by only involving those that are necessary at the appropriate times.

The best way to implement a RACI matrix is to confirm that each task has a designated individual fulfilling the role. It is possible that more than one role is given to the same individual but this should only be limited to roles that are not vital and are not difficult to complete.

To keep things stress-free and simple, each task should only have one person in the "accountable" section, even though it is okay to share responsibilities if it is necessary.

If many individuals are involved in the "consulted" category, it is essential to evaluate and confirm whether all the individuals are necessary. Those that are not vital to the "consulted" category can be moved to the "informed" category to save time in communication.

A RACI matrix is an excellent tool to use for project management that makes it easier for teams to communicate and complete a project at a much faster pace.

PDPC

PDPC Process Decision Program Chart is used to create contingency plans. The primary objective of PDPC is to identify the consequential impact of failure on activity plans, projects and create appropriate contingency plans to limit or mitigate risks. PDPC is often added to process map and tree diagrams to identify failure modes, consequences of those failures and possible countermeasures.

Arrow Diagram

Arrow Diagram or Activity Diagrams are graphical representations of the workflow. It is a form of Flowchart. Activity diagrams depict stepwise activities, actions, and roles along with number of frequency and concurrency. Arrows run from the start towards the end and represent the order in which tasks or activities happen.

Kamishibai Boards

Kamishibai Boards are a series of cards placed on a board and selected at random or per schedule by supervisors, managers, and auditors of the area. This ensures safety and cleanliness of the workplace are maintained and that quality checks are performed regularly.

Kamishibai known as paper drama is a form of storytelling that originated in Japanese Buddhist temples in the 12th Century. This technique was later implemented by Toyota in their production system as a means of visual control for performing audits within a manufacturing process.

Kamishibai Boards may be used as a vital tool while implementing the 5S business process improvement methodology. They also help perform mini-audits during Gemba. Kamishibai board includes - a planning board, T-cards with one green and one red side, an attendance list to see who has performed the audit and a 3C list (concern, cause, and countermeasure) on which the reason or an occurring red outcome and the countermeasures are written.

The Kamishibai planning board has two columns. Unused T-cards are placed on its left side, while audit results are placed on the right end. Each T-card contains a title, such as Kaizen or 5S, with a few simple questions, the auditor may ask the shop floor employee or at a workstation. Both sides of the T-card are identical except for their color.

The attendance sheet is kept to document the details of the individual doing the Kamishibai audit. It also shows who regularly visits the Gemba (meaning workplace) and who possibly needs extra training to make him or her more comfortable going to the Gemba and do an audit.

Kamishibai Boards facilitate Gemba walks. During an audit, when responses are correct, the T card is placed with green side up, while an incorrect reply receives a red card. The details of deviation are recorded on the 3C list (concern, cause, and countermeasure) along with recommendations to prevent such deviation from re-occurring.

When a person does not work per standard, there are three possibilities- First, the employee is not informed about the correct way of working and therefore needs training. Second, the details about standard have not been explained to the worker or the defined standard may be wrong. The third possibility, the employee constantly and intentionally deviates from company policies. This demands strict disciplinary action for the continuous improvement momentum to continue and grow.

Kamishibai Boards also help check that continuous improvement efforts are sustained and that employees do not slip back into their old ways of working.

5W+1H

5W + 1H Kaizen Tool		
What?	**Who?**	**When?**
What to do?	Who does it?	When to do it?
What must be done?	Who must do it?	When is, it done?
What is being done?	Who else can do it?	When should it be done?
What else can be done?	Who is doing it?	When else can it be done?
What else must be done?		When should it not be done?
What else should have been done?		
What must not be done?		
Where?	**Why?**	**How?**
Where to do it?	Why do it?	How to do it?
Where is, it being done?	Why do they do it?	How has it been done?
Where should it be done?	Why do it at all?	How is it being done?
Where else can it be done?	Why do it this way?	How can/should it be done?
Where else should it be done?	Why not do it this way?	How can this be used else
	Why are they doing it?	where?
	Why shouldn't it be done?	How can it be done differently?

Few of the questions under this tool include:

- ✓ What is the purpose of the process?
- ✓ Who is responsible for the tasks?
- ✓ What is the capacity or throughput?
- ✓ What are current bottlenecks of the value stream?
- ✓ How does information flow in the company (both upstream and downstream)?
- ✓ How are employees trained, motivated, empowered?
- ✓ How are our vendors integrated with operations?
- ✓ How do materials reach various manufacturing stages?
- ✓ How does line balancing happen?

None of these questions must be answered in yes or no. Elaborate data must be provided against each question.

Value Stream Mapping

Value Stream Mapping is done to record, evaluate and map workflow of a business. A fully loaded VSM looks like a Kanban board. Value stream map must be pictured and displayed with all recorded data, work logs, backlog, frequency etc. to easily spot areas of improvement. It focuses on cycle time, lead times, throughput and flow efficiency of business processes, therefore is the tool of choice to identify process 'hidden' inefficiencies.

It is a technique that solely uses pen and paper to gain insight and understanding of the movement of information or materials through the value stream that contributes to the production of a product. It is a tool that is most frequently used in Lean Kaizen approaches along with process mapping.

Value stream analysis differs from process mapping since it collects and shows a much larger range of information, involves more processes, used in wider circumstances and is used to find out where the focus of future events should be placed. Different products and/ or departmental work processes may have different value stream maps. Hence, each of them must be mapped independently end- to-end.

Also, referred to as an 'end-to-end' map, value stream analysis does not only use the information regarding various activities leading up to a product, but also incorporates other elements of the entire process such as information and management methods.

It is an excellent tool for lowering time within a sequence since it allows one to find out valuable information regarding the process of making decisions as well as the actual process itself. Instead of jumping into value stream analyses in one go, it is wiser to start implementing it in segments instead. This can also help to reduce the initial costs that it can take to start implementing the changes involved post value stream analysis.

The two main stages of constructing a value stream analysis are to map out the various stages in the process itself and conclude that information by placing a map above with the flow of information that is involved in the process.

All the activities involved in the creation of a product are listed in value stream analysis. This makes it easier to view the difference between meaning and necessary activities against those that are a waste of time or are prone to error.

A good example of a value stream analysis makes it easy to separate the time by dividing activities that are deemed valuable and non-valuable. The analysis will make it clear as to which processes can be improved and can also be used to solve a specific problem, such as- find out where to focus efforts to waste reduction in a production facility.

Once type, number, and extent of waste/ inefficiencies are identified, the next step is to establish goals for improvement and the roadmap to get there.

Here are few insights and answers for commonly asked questions around Kaizen ...

Thought Leader Insights

"Why Kaizen? Will it bring about a change?" Such and similar questions are very common ...

Yes. Kaizen is an excellent change management tool. However, Kaizen works with small minimal increments, hence change happens slowly.

Kaizen is a marathon, not a sprint...

Business today demands improvements fast-everything is wanted today, if not yesterday! Also, if survival of the business itself is the question, then initiating Kaizen will not help. Aggressive change management techniques (discussed in next chapter) must be employed to first bring about change; then use Kaizen to sustain it.

Old employees (old not in age, but tenure within the organization) mostly tend to voice such statements. As change management experts, business leaders, we need to focus on doing what is right for the business rather than complying with heritage employee whims.

In fact, I would recommend that 'adaptability assessment' must be used as a metric while hiring new talent. The continuous improvement and/or Kaizen program should be tied to Human Resources and Talent Management procedures.

Another important point to assess is to question- Is change necessary? Are we thinking about change because everyone else is going for it, or is it because there are evident customer trends, financial logic, want to create product USP (Unique Selling Point) or any other empirical evidence?

While we plan for change, it is worthwhile to know where the existing processes came from.

Why existing process became what they are? Change for the sake of change is counterproductive.

True change can't happen unless the entire employee force (old and new) participates fully. Hence, bringing awareness about the potential benefit of proposed change is a vital requirement of Kaizen.

"We find the same problems every other morning. Can Kaizen bring a change?"

Yes, Kaizen can bring a change to recurring problems. But, first let us understand what usually gets done with regularly occurring problems? My best guess is, most of the time, the pesky issue is tackled for the day, allowing it to re-occur the next day.

Questioning "Why" is it happening in a repeating pattern, will help get to the seat of the problem. The key to effective change management is to know what the root cause of the pain is. Is the problem due to- unplanned work, work overload or company's culture of 'daily firefighting'?

Senior management usually fails to consider why the fire is created. On the other hand, employees might be unwilling to remedy the situation for fear of losing their jobs. A daily fire-to-fight at hand keeps everyone busy (and employed).

*If you always do what you have
always done, you will always get
what you have always got!*

If you do not want to deal with the same problems daily, determine the root cause, focus on prevention of the problem, reward the right things, and change the company's culture from hero-ing firefighters to a culture of bettering consistently. And, Kaizen can bring about such a change.

Take-a-Five

Take five minutes to think and jot down answers to the following questions-

- Do you deal with a daily occurring pesky problem at your workplace?
- What do you think should be done to change it?

When do we initiate Kaizen in an organization?

Kaizen is a business lifestyle and must be practiced in all areas of the organization. Answers to following questions must be looked into before initiating Kaizen:

- Is your organization process healthy?
- Are processes within the company stable?

Because, if the business is traversing through pressing issues such as keeping its head above water, poor cash-flow, high rejects, a high number of product returns, poor throughput, backorders etc. the problem itself must be fixed prior to initiating Kaizen. Such process improvements are known as 'Breakthrough Improvements'.

A quick technique is to plot a control chart for process outcome (result) Vs time. Check for deviations if any and the frequency of such occurrences with Histogram. Run a Root cause analysis and establish if the deviations are because of 'common cause' or 'special cause' variations. For 'special cause' incidents use CAPA (Corrective Action Preventive Action). For all other incidents, initiate Breakthrough Improvement campaign.

Some of the Breakthrough Improvement techniques which can be successfully implemented in pharmaceutical, medical device and biotech industries are Lean Six Sigma, Six Sigma, ISO, Theory of Constraints (TOC), Balanced Score Card etc. The choice of these techniques will primarily depend on the organization's size, budget and number of processes to be re-designed. Once the 'problem' process has been fixed, Kaizen (Make Better) must start immediately.

Take-a-Five

Take five minutes to think and jot down answers for the following questions-

- Is the business going through a rough patch and processes need a re-design?

- What are the different 'special cause' and 'common cause' variations found at your workplace?
- How many and at what frequency do these variations occur?

How do we initiate Kaizen in an organization?

To achieve success with process improvements efforts via Kaizen, a culture of Kaizen needs to be first created within the company.

If a thing's worth doing, it's worth doing well. - Chinese proverb

---

Coming up in the next chapter, we will look at- How to create a Kaizen culture in your organization...

Chapter 5: Creating Kaizen culture

In this chapter, we will see ...

- ✓ Success criteria for Kaizen culture.

- ✓ Kaizen Strategy Model.

- ✓ Kaizen Leader.

- ✓ Kaizen Promotion Office.

- ✓ Change Management Essentials.

- ✓ Culture Checklist.

- ✓ Thought Leader Insights.

Shruti Bhat

Culture means we all smile in the same language.

A group of people working together as in a company create a working principle, practice, and process; then there are some unspoken rules, together they set a company's culture...

To introduce Kaizen in a start-up hence is much easier as against established businesses. This is not because of a start-up's size, but more so because the work culture in a start-up is forming and malleable. It is also comparatively easy to introduce changes to the few members working in a start-up.

It is a mammoth job of bringing on anything new in established companies, big or small.

For established firms, I would recommend going in for time-tested Change Management models, customized to benefit your company's core values and business landscape. I will elaborate on Change Management models later in this chapter. Driving organizational change is an important activity vital for successful implementation of business improvement methodology.

"The secret to getting ahead is getting started. The secret of getting started is breaking your complex overwhelming tasks into small manageable tasks and starting on the first one." -Mark Twain

'Kaizen is not just one's, but everybody's business within a company'- is the fundamental principle of Kaizen methodology. Hence, success with Kaizen happens when entire workforce within the company is geared up to implement change.

Some people are hard-wired to accept change; others may be apprehensive, indecisive or even downright opposed to the prospect of change. Effective communication about Kaizen methodology, the company's rationale behind embracing Kaizen, its potential benefits will progressively shift natural resistors towards Kaizen goals.

Tip: It is critical to classify employees based on their Kaizen acceptance spectrum.

Organizational change is a structured approach for ensuring that changes are smoothly and successfully implemented to achieve lasting benefits and make the organization more efficient, effective and profitable. Simply telling people how to employ Kaizen in their work will be fruitless. Employees must be actively engaged in the entire process of Kaizen campaign design and its implementation.

Therefore, 'Hello *XYZ*,' type of emails won't reach even the first base of employee engagement. People engagement happens when people are involved in the total Kaizen process and explain succinctly-

✓ Here is what our Kaizen initiative is all about ...

✓ Kaizen is important to the company because ...

✓ This is when we plan to go ahead with the Kaizen initiative ...

✓ These are our Kaizen success metrics ...

✓ This is what the company needs you to do and how...

✓ This is what company will do for you/ Kaizen implementation ...

Success with Kaizen success happens when people integrate scientific thinking with Kaizen format to solve daily problems at their workplaces.

Let's understand success criteria for creating a Kaizen culture in an organization ...

Success Criteria for Kaizen culture

Following are several enablers for a Kaizen culture. Kaizen facilitators should conduct frequent assessment around them-

Objective

If a company desires that its employees embrace Kaizen (i.e. make better consistently) then, the true benefits of Kaizen must be explained to them. Simply stating 'profits to company', 'growth' etc. will not matter to employees of 21st Century business. The reason being, employees of yester-years stayed with one employer for their entire work life; perhaps even retired with a gold watch. Today, job security is a gone thing, so is employee loyalty.

To make Kaizen a success, employees must be told 'what is in it for them'

Flexible strategy roadmap

Gone are those days when business strategies were planned for 3 to 5 years as a part of a long-term corporate vision. Today, companies both large and small, witness daily change- be it economic, demographic, ecological, consumer habits, consumer's buying power, government regulations, competition, intellectual property walls or a key employee resigning. Business strategies must be effective and agile to deal with such daily change.

Further, accomplishing every short-term and long-term goal is vital for a company's survival. This must be explained to employees on a regular basis. When people feel included in business decisions, feeling of ownership evolves, which will drive decisions into potential successes.

Long-term vision

Any change to business process brings on a business transformation. The extent of transformation will depend on type and rate of change as well as the improvement methodology used.

Kaizen shows results with small increments done consistently all the time. Hence, it would be unrealistic to expect astounding results at the drop of the hat. Company's senior leadership and employees must be made aware that, their time, money and efforts are being put into a methodology that guarantees best returns, however, the pace will be slow. Further, everyone needs to show patience and perseverance to gain full potential of Kaizen benefits.

Shared vision

Kaizen campaigns must not be sub-optimized to a specific location or department of the company. Kaizen is a holistic approach, even if it were to be applied to a department or just one business process within the company. Process changes at one part of business give dividends to everyone in the company. To accomplish success with Kaizen, awareness, and information about Kaizen must transcend to all layers within the company. Kaizen promotes 'how can I help you (all) to help me?" approach rather than 'I will simply do my job'.

Continuous communication

For Kaizen to kick-off the ground, there must be continuous communication.

Communication channels should be established within the company, based on what works best for the company and its employees. Creating a Kaizen promotion office is a helpful way of ensuring fruitful communication. I shall elaborate on Kaizen promotion office later in this chapter.

Quality-by-design

Concept of quality, its significance, and awareness of its importance to business success has evolved over few decades. Pharmaceutical, medical device, and biotech industries introduced good manufacturing practices (GMP) after the infamous thalidomide babies case several decades ago and suffixed it with a 'c' to always keep it 'current'.

Quality goes into the product via its facility, processes and design principles.

Applying Kaizen to product development not only introduces quality-by-design into products, but also helps R&D departments to eliminate formulation errors, shorten development timelines, and give out higher number of products at less cost!

Being fearless

Ability to take risks is a primary criterion for success be it R&D, finance, operations or any other quarter of the company. The risks, however, must be appropriately managed to minimize losses.

To create Kaizen culture, it is imperative to foster an environment of fearlessness, so employees are comfortable to speak their mind about any potential pitfalls that they might envisage. There must be a healthy dialog to evaluate all points of apprehension from any employee at any time. Discussion forums must be appropriately scheduled so everyone can participate in the debate. Kaizen strategy roadmaps must evolve organically from within the company rather than someone telling people 'what to do'.

Transparent leadership

As with fearlessness, another common trait 'blame-game' must be totally removed, for Kaizen to sustain. High amount of transparency in Kaizen decision-making and visual management must be practiced as a part of corporate governance.

Visual management means that information is constantly visible, easily available and manageable at all times to all employees. Information displayed on the company intranet, bulletin boards, social media, Kaizen newsletters, interaction with members of Kaizen promotion office etc. are few examples how companies may foster visual management.

Ownership and employee empowerment

Each employee based on their position on the company ladder influences and creates a culture change. Not many people in the organization truly are aware of the good and/or bad influence they exert on their surrounding and the impact on company's culture.

A prerequisite of Kaizen culture is that employees are properly trained about expected contributions viz. ideas, strategy roadmaps, implementation and sustaining Kaizen. Ownership gives them authority while training tells them about their duties, responsibility, and accountability.

Collaborative approach

Improving the culture, work processes and work systems in a company is everybody's job. Kaizen is therefore one-hundred percent teamwork.

Each Kaizen proposal must accompany a rationale and potential benefit to the organization. No one expects people to say "Yes" all the time. In fact, saying "No" must be encouraged.

However, dissuade saying "No" for the sake of obstructing. Every 'No' must be justified. All decisions must involve all employees like an 'open house' session where everyone can voice their affirmations and concerns.

The underlying principle of Kaizen is 'respect for people'.

At the outset, the Kaizen team must, therefore, set up clear boundaries, constraints, guidelines, goals, roadmaps about how ideas must be collected, presented, maintain decorum and discuss matters in a non-confrontational, professional and collaborative style.

Training

Employees should not be simply sent to training programs and several training hours documented. What matters are not the hours of training, but what people learn- theory and skills. The worst possible environment for developing skill is a classroom. The best possible environment is at the Gemba. For example, if one wants to learn lawn tennis they don't sit in an air-conditioned classroom and watch the instructor swing a racket; they would go to the tennis court i.e. the Gemba.

To give Kaizen learners a framework and push, conduct a little bit of training in the classroom and then immediately hit the Gemba. A formal structured Kaizen course must have intensive training along with a process improvement project. The student is coached, monitored and evaluated continuously to teach the next lesson, next skill, so learning itself becomes a continuous process of self-development.

Rewards and recognition

Rewards and recognition should happen in a fair and just fashion, as per pre-established guidelines. It is very common to see smart employees quietly leave organizations if they believe their contributions didn't receive appropriate appreciation. I shall elaborate on this topic in the next chapter on implementing Kaizen.

Take-a-Five

Take five minutes to think and jot down answers to the following questions-

- Do you feel like an 'empowered' employee?
- Does your company culture promote learning, self-motivation and collaborative work style?
- Is your company culture tremendously politically afflicted i.e. do you feel there is too much of office politics?
- Are there too many 'blame games' happening in your workplace?
- Is there a rewards & recognition policy document within your company? If so, are you and other employees satisfied with it? What changes would you like to see in that document?

The Kaizen enabler points help is establishing 'desired state of Kaizen' which is the company's Goal.

Tip: Kaizen creates a constant flow of process improvement ideas. Many of those ideas would never get started or implemented without Kaizen.

Each new idea is a small step in the right direction of continuing process of improvement. Over time those numerous small steps add up to provide substantial benefits to your company.

Kaizen assumes that the 'show must go on' even while the improvements are taking place within a company. This keeps productivity up each day while preparing for better productivity for the next one.

Kaizen Strategy Planning Model

The fundamental principle of Kaizen strategy design is to bring about 'Continuing Improvement' using incremental improvement day-to-day to realize big gains.

While it is true that continuous improvement of candles didn't result in the electric bulb i.e. a breakthrough invention was necessary. The other side of the tale is- Implementing Kaizen can't come up with a 'better way' of doing business, but a 'better way' of doing business can definitely be improved via Kaizen. Applying Kaizen to day-to-day business working is the key to success!

If you don't plan to succeed, you plan to fail. And all big journeys start with a small step. Kaizen strategy planning is designing a plan for 'Improving the way you improve'.

The first step to creating Kaizen culture is Strategic Planning Model. This model has three tiers.

Tier 1 is the company's senior management. Tier 1's role and goal are to introduce Kaizen as a corporate strategy, provide the vision, mission, dollars and directional leadership. Further, they provide the tools and facilitate information about why a change is needed? How can Kaizen help? What Kaizen does? They also set milestones and performance metrics for Kaizen campaign.

Tip: Value stream mapping and other tools may be used to identify areas of improvement, while quality, cost, delivery (takt time) and motivation (QCDM) comprise performance metrics.

"Sans a clearly defined strategic plan, Kaizen campaign is a long shot"

- Dr. Shruti Bhat

Tier 2 is the middle management. Tier 2 designs strategic implementation and continuous monitoring of Kaizen campaign.

Tier 3 comprises all other employees. They engage in small groups and collaborative activities to bring on Kaizen as a part of daily working. Success with Kaizen happens when all three tiers synchronize consistently.

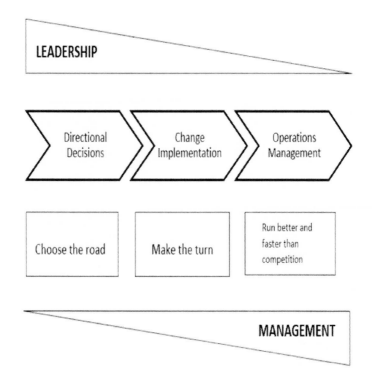

A dedicated team comprising representatives from all three tiers must be formed, with a committed Kaizen leader. The team should be given a designated area for working usually referred as 'Kaizen Promotion Office'.

Kaizen promotion office is responsible for creating and sustaining Kaizen culture within the company.

Kaizen Leader

"To do great things is difficult, but to command great things is more difficult." – Friedrich Nietzsche

Requirements of a Kaizen Leader/ Director:

- Knowledge of Kaizen and/or Lean or Lean Six Sigm.
- Knowledge of responsibilities.
- Develop training programs.
- Skill in instructing to coach and/or mentor employees.
- Skill in process improvement.
- Skill in working with people, team building, and conflict control.
- Skill in effectively communicating change over time.

"To a person who does not know where he wants to go, there is no favorable wind."

– Lucius Annaeus Seneca

Choose a person irrespective of the title or position in the organization. A Kaizen leader must-

- Inspire everyone to Kaizen philosophies.
- Analyze current situation and set vision, mission, and goals for creating a Kaizen culture.
- Motivate employees and steer everyone into achieving Kaizen goals.
- Oversees training of employees to bring on awareness about Kaizen campaign.
- Create strategic roadmaps for bringing on Kaizen culture and oversee their implementation.
- Motivate and empower employees to contribute, participate and sustain Kaizen.

There are multiple roles of a Kaizen leader. Kaizen leader is an evangelist, change agent, champion, and manager. Kaizen leader can be a single individual with multiple hats; usually found in startups and small businesses.

Mid-size and bigger organizations assign Kaizen leadership role to a small team of individuals usually a mix of internal employees and external consultants.

155

Kaizen evangelist is the innovator, the brain behind the mission. Evangelists are self-starters and self-motivators, knowledge experts who read books on Kaizen, attend conferences, keep themselves up-to-date with information and bring new ideas to the company. They also coach and train people, deal with skeptics and make Kaizen information available to everyone in the company.

Kaizen change agents are the early adopters and influence others to bring on Kaizen culture. They get things in motion, facilitate events, maintain momentum, support Kaizen leaders and sustain Kaizen culture.

Kaizen champions lead and drive change. They are change agents in company's leadership team. They are transformational leaders and provide resources for Kaizen culture to root-in and blossom. They help evangelists, change agents and other committed employees to promote Kaizen awareness. They remove obstructions; respond to critics, skeptics as well as genuine queries about Kaizen. They create a cross-departmental framework for creating Kaizen culture and companywide implementation of Kaizen.

Kaizen manager is anyone who leads Kaizen within the company. They are not managerial positions with titles but are functional roles. They are not the conventional 'boss' or 'department heads' rather are role models for creating and sustaining Kaizen.

The picture below illustrates skill set of a Kaizen leader-

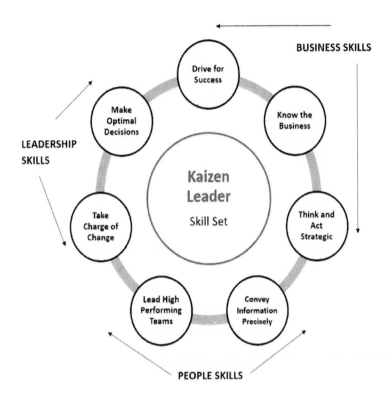

Kaizen Promotion Office

A big part of the Kaizen process is implementing change over and over and over again. Creating the office, choosing a Kaizen leader and team members is the next step in Kaizen campaign implementation.

I briefly touched upon Kaizen promotion office in the previous chapter. Unlike other offices, Kaizen promotion office Head need not be a member from company's senior leadership team. The individual's title and designation within the company are unimportant. The most critical and only attribute necessary is the ability to influence people and drive them towards a common goal.

"A leader is a dealer in hope."-
Napoléon Bonaparte

Characteristics of a Kaizen Promotion Office (KPO) team:

- The team must have members representing various departments across the company.
- The members must have good inter-personal relations and the ability to work together towards a common goal.
- The members must have ability to contribute, lead and work with others.

The Kaizen promotion office team members provide administrative analytical and technical support to the areas within the company that is involved in Kaizen activities. Here's a typical position summary of a KPO associate to help you build your team.

Kaizen Promotion Office Associate (position summary):

This position is responsible for facilitating the implementation of Kaizen campaign by providing administrative and analytical support, as well as technical assistance to the areas within the organization that is involved in Kaizen activities.

Essential job functions:

- Provide Kaizen activity tracking and support. Collect and centralize Kaizen activity measures, re-measures and make them accessible to the transformation guiding team and value stream sponsor team.

- Analyze the data pertaining to the Kaizen activities and create visuals/ dashboards that can be presented at leadership team and administrative team meetings.

- Customize and standardize the electronic materials and tool kits, required to successfully run Kaizen events including training.

- Work with the KPO Director to develop and design production boards and provide technical assistance to other areas, help in completing data collection, reporting assignments and other tasks as needed.

- Work with the KPO Director to create, design, and maintain companny-wide Kaizen skills map.

- Develop routine communication (via identified channels) to educate and update staff on Kaizen progress. Works with KPO Director to determine how messages are disseminated.

- Schedule and coordinate meetings with internal as well as external clients pre- and post-Kaizen events.

- Setup and coordinate training sessions and events preceding as well as following the training.

Education and Experience:

Bachelor's degree in Business Administration or Pharmaceutical Management or Healthcare Administration or a related field with 1 to 2 years of experience. Work exposure to conducting BA/ BE, clinical studies, formulation R&D and/or CRO management is preferred. Certification with Lean or Lean Six Sigma practices is preferred.

Computer Skills:

This position must demonstrate an operating knowledge of computers. This position must have intermediate level ability with Word-processing, Emailing and intermediate to advanced level ability to work with Spreadsheets. Project Management expertise will be an asset.

Continuing improvement with Kaizen requires a bottom-up continuous stream of communication.

Things are always changing in a Kaizen oriented facility. How can everyone stay up to date?

Inefficiencies and problems with processes will be felt across the company. For example, an inefficient tableting process may hold-up production for a product, as well as other products on the shop floor.

This could result in pending production, backorders and stress to IPQC, testing lab and quality assurance teams. This pain is referred on R&D team, since they would be summoned to provide a solution to this mess. The pain also gets referred to logistics, sales, and marketing teams, as they must deal with inquiries of product shortages in the market, hardships to patients, risk of product substitution by competing brands, loss in market share, loss in reputation, loss in revenue, etc.

The point I am driving at is that, because the effect of a problem is felt by everyone, it is in everyone's interest to support process improvement efforts technical or otherwise. The nature, scope, and extent of difficulties felt must be efficiently captured. Who else but the employees affected by the pain would best know how severe the pain is, isn't it?

Usually, people at the site of such pain are on the lowermost ladder of company structure and have the best information about the process and potential ideas for improvement. Collecting their comments and feedback is vital for Kaizen's success. This transparency, openness and approach of involving employees right at the outset, also reduces the possibility of resistance. Early-stage employee involvement helps bring about process ownership and employee empowerment. It is an accepted norm that, not everyone will contribute to the same extent, but incremental improvement is certainly within everyone's ability.

Kaizen culture begins with creating a Kaizen promotion office (KPO). In startups and small to mid-size companies, the KPO is usually facilitated by an external consultant. Larger organizations typically select a couple of employees, train them on Kaizen philosophies and have them lead the campaign.

The KPO is driven by Kaizen leader, evangelists and change agents who educate employees about Kaizen, its benefits, implementation challenges and success techniques. Employees must be completely out of their 'job-loss fear mode' for Kaizen to take-off the ground. A vital point which must be explained to all employees at the kick-off of Kaizen campaign is that-

Kaizen = Respect for people = No layoffs due to Kaizen

Besides training and informing, the Kaizen promotion office issues Kaizen newspaper or newsletter, periodically to update everyone on the campaigns progress and collect ideas via Kaizen cards. Suggestions from these cards are then looped into the campaign and the Kaizen cycle continues...

Tip: Pharmaceuticals inherently have strictest quality standards and as these standard change, improvements happen, so why Kaizen?

It must be noted that **Kaizen not equal to Continuous Improvement**.

Tip: Kaizen is 'making better' which is vastly different from continuous improvement. Continuous improvement is external to a process, while Kaizen is internal to a process. For example, a new equipment introduction to the facility is continuous improvement, but it is not Kaizen.

Kaizen is self-development of systems, processes, employees and the company.

Change for better is Kaizen.
Continuous improvement is not the
definition of Kaizen. Rather,
continuous improvement is a result of
Kaizen.

Tip: Japanese literal translation of Continuous Improvement is Keizoku-teki Kaizen.

Change Management Essentials

Myth: We don't have a firm plan yet, when do we inform everyone (about the change)?

Response: There is a fine line of demarcation: telling everything upfront to everyone Vs planning process changes behind a wall of secrecy. Employees always appreciate open and interactive approach. It is very much possible to have a frank dialogue with your people giving correct information while maintaining integrity and relevant secrecy. Change should be told with tact...

Getting organizational change right

The picture below gives some of the factors commonly found responsible for failures at implementing change management programs within companies.

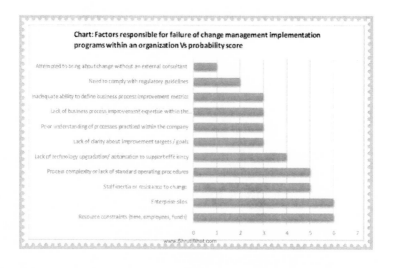

Chart: Factors responsible for failure of change management implementation programs within an organization Vs probability score

Tip: Change is a constant and necessary part of continually improving an organization.

Effective Change Management stages are:

i. Identify need for change.
ii. Develop a strategy and process for change (including mission, associated risks, resources budget and communication).
iii. Communicate the vision and mission for change.
iv. Conduct A/B testing of the change process.
v. Roll out the change process effectively. Monitor the change process and fine tune as required.

Several change management techniques are available. However, I have found Kotter's 8-step change model, Lewin change management model, ADKAR model, and McKinsey 7S model bring rich success.

Kotter's 8-step change model

The model comprises of-

Step 1: Create urgency for change.

Step 2: Form a powerful coalition.

Step 3: Create a vision for change.

Step 4: Communicate the vision.

Step 5: Remove obstacles.

Step 6: Create short-term wins.

Step 7: Build on the change.

Step 8: Secure the changes firmly within the corporate culture.

Lewin's change management model

The model comprises of-

Step 1: Unfreeze, that is, break down the existing status quo.

Step 2: Transition after the change.

Step 3: Refreeze, which means, making sure that the 'changes' get used all the time and that they are incorporated into everyday business.

ADKAR change management model

The model suggests that 'change' requires managing five key goals-

Goal 1: **A**wareness of the need to change.

Goal 2: **D**esire to participate and support the change.

Goal 3: **K**nowledge of how to change (and what the change looks like).

Goal 4: **A**bility to implement the change on a routine basis.

Goal 5: **R**einforcement to keep the changes consistent.

Prosci 3 phase change management process:

Phase1: Preparing for change (preparedness, assessment, and strategy development).

Phase 2: Managing change (detailed planning and change management implementation).

Phase 3: Reinforcing change (data gathering, corrective action, recognition).

McKinsey 7S change management model

McKinsey's model examines an organization as a collection of business flows with a critical link between operational drivers and strategic success.

Apropos this model, seven core elements often referred as Seven Ss are needed to evaluate businesses, and find out what processes are effective and which are not. In order to gain an advantage, businesses must focus on all seven elements simultaneously, since they are inter-related. Any change to one of the seven elements will have a ripple effect over the remaining six elements.

7S model includes-

S1: *Strategy,* refers to the proposal that is created to sustain and improve business processes against its competitors.

S2: *Structure,* is the approach that the organization is arranged concerning ranking and how issues should be reported and to whom.

S3: *Systems,* incorporates the daily processes that employees are required to participate in order to complete the task.

S4: *Shared values,* otherwise known as super-ordinate goals, are the company's key values that are evident in the culture of the corporation and general work approach.

S5: *Staff,* refers to all the company's employees and what they are capable of.

S6: *Skill* implies the skills and proficiencies of the company's staff.

S7: *Style,* refers to the entire spectrum of corporate governance.

A major advantage of the 7S model is that, it is applicable to any industry, type or size of teams. On the other hand, it has a major limitation as well, that is, unless appropriately handled, this model can exhibit higher failure rates.

Next phase of business process improvement campaign is to clearly define and express expectations to employees. For example- it is common for expectations to include punctual employees, attendance at gatherings, timely completion of project milestones, timely submission of project data etc.

Employees ought to know their contributions are greatly appreciated and respected. Questions, feedback, and ideas are just some of the many ways that employees can contribute to business improvement program.

Using a variety of assessment tools, such as tests, observations or reviews, one can assess employee's improvement. Assessing improvement should be done frequently to make sure that individuals are on the right track. It is also a good gauge of knowing whether learning sessions should be increased or if other skills should be focused on, instead.

Tip: Selecting appropriate change model is vital for successful business process improvement campaign.

Tip: Ideal change model for an organization would be dependent on the size of organization, depth & extent of prevailing organizational politics, the types & number of business process 'problem areas' and the business improvement technique.

Tip: To know what not to do, use SIPOC diagrams.

Tip: Use your analytical skills to select change agents, team members to involve in the planning process.

Resistance Management

Resistance management is a significant aspect of planning and managing change.

General employee types:

- Employees don't acknowledge that a problem exists or they simply choose to overlook them.

- Employees accept that a problem exists, but they choose to live with the issue without doing anything to resolve it.

- Employees accept that a problem exists, however they find excuses for not solving instead of finding ways to resolve the problem.

- Employees are vigilant about potential problems and keep themselves updated on ways of problem solving. Such employees are very willing to participate in the change process.

Several years ago, I was driving my first Kaizen campaign in a R&D division at a client site. On day-1, the very first comment that came my way was- *"It's no use, Kaizen will never work in this company"!*

Take-a-Five

Have you often heard something like this in your department? Please take five minutes to jot down that incident.

Typically, the workforce can be split into four main categories:

- **Change enthusiast:** These are people who dislike maintaining status quo. They always like to take risks and seek new heights.

- **2C Profile-ist:** This comprises majority people who are comfortable with status quo. However, with coaching and convincing (2C) will tend to be supportive and accept moderate changes.

- **Followers:** This group don't have any specific opinion. They simply tend to follow the majority route per se.

- **Naysayers:** These people constantly pose discouraging comments and excuses at every instant new idea are presented. In an economic era where continuous improvement and innovation are a lifeline for businesses, such 'Naysayers' might turn out to be more dreadful than an under-performer.

Here're few methods I've found to be extremely effective to handle Kaizen-killers:

- Demonstrate the damage they cause. Stop excuses and limit destructive criticism.

- Always have a widely-understood system-wide business process.

- Tie 'Kaizen' to 'Company strategy'.

- Spend enough resources on training and coaching Kaizen teams.

- Create an 'Idea management system': if necessary, use external experts to evaluate 'Ideation concepts' before allotting dollars.

- Anchor the changes in corporate culture i.e. make change stick around.

Tip: Kaizen is a continuing improvement process i.e. there is no end date.

Tip: Don't make the mistake of going for the whole transformation too quickly: one of the most common pieces of advice you'll get from all Kaizen experts is 'don't make your Kaizen scope too big'. Even if you have a clear image of where you want to be in the future, it's better to agree that it will take more time than you expect. That way, you can focus your short-term efforts on the first step toward the full implementation of the desired state.

Take-a-Five

Take five minutes to think about these questions and to write down your answers:

- Does your top management usually support new ideas from its employees?

- Do you think you would like to participate in a Kaizen event?

- What are the channels of communication in your company (including grapevine)?

- Where is new information about company's plans, happening, deals etc. posted at your workplace?

- Do you have a company newsletter? If so, what is the frequency of its release?

Tip: Kaizen creates value. If you are a company with two or more production sites you can improve both market share and profit margins through continuing implementation of Kaizen. Also, Kaizen and Lean are often confused and seen as one, but in reality, they are distinct. Lean is a goal to be achieved i.e. total elimination of waste, while Kaizen is the tool used to achieve Lean.

Myth: Kaizen is expensive.

Response: Kaizen adapts common sense to real life situations. It requires little investments and focusses on reducing both material and labor waste. If you have safety, quality or productivity improvement targets then, Kaizen is your time-tested tool!

Kaizen culture checklist

This Kaizen culture checkup checklist consists of 19 questions on corporate culture, infrastructure set up and work tasks, to help you baseline current scenario and highlight areas and opportunities for improvement.

Corporate Culture:

'We have in-house cross-functional teams providing effective solutions'. How does your company fair on this scale? (select one)

☐ Always

☐ Often

☐ Sometimes

☐ Rarely

☐ Never

'Our organization usually raises the bar of excellence by the recruiting new hires'. How does your company fair on this scale? (select one)

☐ Always

☐ Often

☐ Sometimes

☐ Rarely

☐ Never

'Our organization is malleable. We adapt to changes quickly'. For your organization, how often is this statement true? (select one)

☐ Always

☐ Often

☐ Sometimes

☐ Rarely

☐ Never

'We regularly redesign our business processes. For your organization'. How often is this statement true? (select one)

☐ Always

☐ Often

☐ Sometimes

☐ Rarely

☐ Never

'Company leadership, stakeholders are supportive to receiving ideas for improvement'. How does your company fair on this scale? (select one)

☐ Always

☐ Often

☐ Sometimes

☐ Rarely

☐ Never

Infrastructure set up

'We have well-defined strategy outlining the who, what, when, how and why of our continuous improvement efforts'. How does your company fair on this scale? (select one)

☐ Always

☐ Often

☐ Sometimes

☐ Rarely

☐ Never

'Our workspaces are traditional, standard and immobile. We usually don't do collaborative working'. How does your company fair on this scale? (select one)

☐ Always

☐ Often

☐ Sometimes

☐ Rarely

☐ Never

'We have a Rewards & Recognition policy that encourages Kaizen'. How does your company fair on this scale? (select one)

☐ Always

☐ Often

☐ Sometimes

☐ Rarely

☐ Never

'We reward people for number of ideas suggested rather than revenues earned and/or costs saved'. How does your company fair on this scale? (select one)

☐ Always

☐ Often

☐ Sometimes

☐ Rarely

☐ Never

'We believe that we don't have time to implement Kaizen in our company'. How does your company fair on this scale? (select one)

☐ Always

☐ Often

☐ Sometimes

☐ Rarely

☐ Never

'We believe that we don't have resources to implement Kaizen in our company'. How does your company fair on this scale? (select one)

☐ Always

☐ Often

☐ Sometimes

☐ Rarely

☐ Never

Work Tasks:

'We generate a lot of ideas, conduct ideas games, ideation and/or design thinking process'. How does your company fair on this scale? (select one)

☐ Always

☐ Often

☐ Sometimes

☐ Rarely

☐ Never

'We constant evolve our employee talents through training and/or real-time project work involving Kaizen'. How does your company fair on this scale? (select one)

☐ Always

☐ Often

☐ Sometimes

☐ Rarely

☐ Never

'We don't work with Kaizen. We have other business process improvement methodologies running in our company'. How does your company fair on this scale? (select one)

☐ Always

☐ Often

☐ Sometimes

☐ Rarely

☐ Never

'We put 'pull' or 'customer demand' at the heart of our company's operations'. How does your company fair on this scale? (select one)

☐ Always

☐ Often

☐ Sometimes

☐ Rarely

☐ Never

'We do exhaustive process benchmarking study at the time of designing business strategies or market expansions'. How does your company fair on this scale? (select one)

☐ Always

☐ Often

☐ Sometimes

☐ Rarely

☐ Never

'We do exhaustive business analysis at the time of designing business strategies'. How does your company fair on this scale? (select one)

☐ Always

☐ Often

☐ Sometimes

☐ Rarely

☐ Never

'Our talent pool is creative and continuously generates 'new' ways of doing things'. How does your company fair on this scale? (select one)

☐ Always

☐ Often

☐ Sometimes

☐ Rarely

☐ Never

'Our talent pool is collaborative and self-motivated'. How does your company fair on this scale? (select one)

☐ Always

☐ Often

☐ Sometimes

☐ Rarely

☐ Never

Results:

80 / 95: Good, your organization is on the right path of Process Improvement.

60 / 95: It is about time to roll out Process Improvement initiatives in your organization. This might look like new products and services or the ability to adapt to changing conditions rapidly. This good thing you have got going will need attention, so consider some Kaizen team coaching to improve your process improvement successes rates. Consider this: what would it look like to move from a good level of improvement to an exceptional level? How might your customers and employees benefit from that level of improvement?

Below 60: Your company's 'Business growth strategies" must be re-designed.

Thought Leader Insights

"Our profits would have been better if our R&D output was up to the mark. How can we bring forth positive transformation in our Research and Development division with Kaizen?"

Response: Employ PDCA tool. For success with R&D process improvements, one needs to spend quality time in the *'design'* or *'plan'* phase. Establish clearly which metric(s) you wish to improve- Is the goal to reduce product formulation errors? Or is the goal to formulate products quicker?

"What are the top technical, people skills one should look for while hiring a Kaizen Expert or Consulting firm?"

Response: There are nine skills of highly effective Continuous Improvement/ Business Process Management Expert, namely:

i.	Ability to understand client's business and be efficient at stakeholder management.
ii.	Should have an integrated and overall understanding of the pharmaceuticals, medical devices industry sector, its peculiarities, regulations & legislations, product types, customer avenues, and marketing geographies. Most importantly for companies, it is imperative to match 'chemistry' with the Expert, rather than looking at 'geometry' of the Consulting firm.
iii.	Up-to-date knowledge of different process management methodologies.
iv.	Passion for implementing them to bring forth the desired positive changes within prescribed time, scope and budget.
v.	Ability to speak up when top management is wrong.
vi.	Ability to explain complex ideas in simple words.
vii.	Ability to listen and openness to learning.
viii.	Patience, persistence, and persuasion while bringing on and/or managing change.
ix.	Amnesia- This is the most vital criteria. The process improvement expert should forget all the good work they did with previous organizations- What worked there may not work in the new place, as each company has its own set of business processes, people, organizational culture, office politics and associated problems thus. The Kaizen or any process improvement expert should have a mindset of always 'starting with a clean slate'.

A brief pause ...

Pointers to creating a Kaizen culture:

- Everyone is a part of change culture.

- Drivers of engagement.

- Make Kaizen Fun!

- Everyone works together.

- Recognize and reward.

- Everyone gets questioned.

- Small successes lead to bigger ones.

- Be a cheerleader ...

Take-a-Five

Take five minutes to think and jot down your answers-

- What are some of the important things you would be concerned about before planning a culture change for Kaizen in your organization?

- Where do you think, you should do your first Kaizen event within your company?

Tip: Add an extra column to note down 'improvement ideas' to the Process Waste Scorecard from the previous chapter. For prioritization, rank order them, viola!

Tip: It is not always essential for organizations to undergo a complete makeover. Effectiveness can be increased in increments, too... use Kaizen.

Tip: There is no short-cut to excellence; Kaizen is the closest corner to that short-cut.

Process Waste Card:

Process Name	Department	9 Types of wastes									*	Final Score	Improvement Ideas
		Over Production	Inventory	Transportation	Waiting	Over Processing	Wasted Motion	Rework	Un-utilized resources	Defects			

*Based on your results from Take-a-Five exercise, add columns as necessary to the above process waste card. Note- attach data such as interview/ survey/ photos, observations from other short Kaizen events, suggestions received etc. Prepare a summary report to help identify the business process problem.

The power of Kaizen:

Use Kaizen to develop people, creativity, innovation, a competitive edge in products and services, shape and spread ideas, bring a turnaround. Go to 'Gemba'...

Coming up in the next chapter- How to implement Kaizen at your organization?

Chapter 6: Implementing Kaizen

In this chapter, we will see ...

- ✓ Pre-Event Activities.

- ✓ Dos and Don'ts at Kaizen Events.

- ✓ Kaizen Project Management and Project Charter.

- ✓ Kaizen Events Classification.

- ✓ Training.

- ✓ Process Stapling.

- ✓ Root Cause Analysis, Idea Prioritization.

- ✓ Process Improvement.

- ✓ Kaizen Event Implementation Quick Reference List.

- ✓ Thought Leader Insights.

Best can be made still better with Kaizen...

Kaizen Implementation Roadmap:

Three phases of Kaizen events:

Phase 1: Planning and pre-event preparation.

Phase 2: Implementation Go-Live! The event itself

Phase 3: Presentation, celebration, and follow-up.

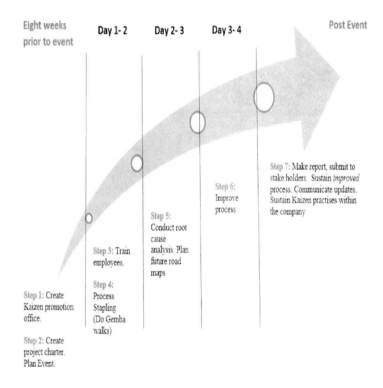

Let us walk through each stage, step-by-step.

*Those who say it cannot be done,
should not interrupt those doing it.*

- Chinese proverb

Pre-Event

Step 1: Create Kaizen Promotion Office

*Business processes work best when
there is input, support and ideas
contributed by various people that are
involved in the organization.*

Modification or improvements to business processes is possible only when people within the organization make business process improvement as their ultimate 'goal'. Company leadership strategizes Kaizen promotion office, assigns goals, and appoints the Kaizen Director who would then build the team to achieve desired goals. The Director also designs the Kaizen work-breakdown structure, cost-breakdown structure, risk-breakdown structure, mitigation strategy as well as the communications strategy.

Kaizen Director Responsibility Checklist:

Pre-event

- Choose/recruit team members.
- Collect background information necessary for the event.
- Ready the area marked out for the event. For example- mark boundaries, tag equipment, rooms, assign roles to people involved in the Kaizen campaign.
- Prepare Kaizen implementation kits and ensure everything that is needed for the event is available.

Note: Event background information includes- applicable standard operating procedures (SOPs), site master file, area maps with swim lanes, process map, process sheets, baseline cycle and takt times, names of personnel & their job responsibilities, equipment IDs with use logs. For manufacturing areas gather details of the product, batch cards, HVAC logs, WIP logs, cleaning records, finished product specifications (FPS), raw material specifications (RMS), In-process quality control (IPQC) data, line clearance logs, raw material, in-process & finished product test reports. Also, collect job training & Kaizen training records of everyone involved with the Kaizen campaign.

During the event (Go live)

- Keep most updated information as happening of the campaign, check whether everyone is doing their roles etc.
- Note takt time and cycle time of process operations.
- Review and approve reports.

Post-event

- Compile slide deck of the presentation and circulate it to company's senior leadership and stakeholders.
- Compile 'follow-up for outstanding items' with roles, responsibilities, and timeline for completion.

Tip: No matter how extensive the Kaizen training, at the implementation site, expect to hear one or many of following statements:

- "We have been doing this way for years and it is working well, why change now"?
- "It sounds nice on paper; I don't think it will work practically"
- "Costs are already as low as they can get ..."
- "We have been doing this job for years; why do we need YOU to tell us what to do"?
- "We simply can't lower costs without compromising quality."
- "Well, everything is going fine, why change?"
- "We tried changing it a few years ago, didn't work ..."

Make sure you have answers ready for each of above. Keep empirical evidence and reports handy wherever possible to support claims.

Dos and don'ts at Kaizen events

- 'How can we do it?' Vs 'Do it yourself'
- 'Sure, we can check for areas to lower costs' Vs 'This is lowest ever cost possible'.
- 'Things can be better' Vs 'This is good enough'.
- 'I will contribute wherever possible' Vs 'I am too busy to do it'.
- 'Kaizen is our collective initiative' Vs 'I have too much work as it is, don't have time for Kaizen'.
- 'Kaizen success is a team effort' Vs 'I made it happen or I did it'.
- 'There is always room for improvement' Vs 'Things are going fine, why change?'

A big part of the Kaizen process is implementing change over and over and over again. Things are always changing in a Kaizen oriented facility. How can everyone stay up to date?

Communication Improvement Plan

Regardless of any improvement activity on-going or under strategic design, periodic updates and work plans must be shared with all employees, senior leadership and stakeholders for the Kaizen practices to continue. Secrecy should not be maintained about Kaizen action plans; transparency is the name of the game for success with Kaizen.

It is critical to use visual communications to inform employees. When a procedure changes, let the affected workers know and create a label at the point of work to remind them of the new process. Change the label when process changes again. Post signs and charts that show the rate of suggestions and the benefits of those changes. Track contributions and announce the next steps.

Kaizen event reports are best communicated using a poster board. List activities completed, results, insights, backlog i.e. list of outstanding items etc. Additional items that could be displayed are- new areas of inefficiency identified, new root causes detected, proposed improvement plans, call for brainstorming sessions, details of suggestions received, actions performed, new member job posting etc.

Channels of communication must be both 'push' and 'pull' based i.e. making information reach your audience and keeping it displayed/ available for anyone who wants to consult/ review Kaizen activity plans, performance etc.

Kaizen wiki page, Kaizen newsletter, Kaizen newspaper, Kaizen forum, Kaizen corner, Kaizen community have proved extremely helpful for rolling, trolling, and sustaining Kaizen.

Kaizen forum is an online forum created to allow discussions to happen on Kaizen activities. Kaizen corner is a designated place, where people could assemble and give short speeches or share their thoughts on Kaizen team's improvement. Kaizen community is a small Kaizen group with a mentor. Several such communities may prevail across various departments within the company. The goal of all Kaizen communities is to support Kaizen promotion office and team goals.

Tip: A mix of offline and online communication techniques yields best results.

Gemba walk is yet another useful channel. It gathers information about problems as they happen. The collected information post-it is displayed on the Kaizen board in that area. Gemba walk also helps audit premises post events.

Traditionally Kaizen principles rely on manual tools than analog or digital tools i.e. to use a pen, pencil, paper, boards instead of digital forms of reporting. Digital tools may be an add-on to manual logs, not a substitute. I would recommend conducting a survey of employee's preference. It helps achieve communication objectives quicker and meets with less employee resistance.

Visual display and visual management are vital. Visibility also brings peer pressure on teams. Hence, if a company decides to go solely digital then all digital data must be displayed on screens placed at designated spots (just as physical Kaizen boards). Just like physical boards, digital boards must be owned by Kaizen promotion office and Kaizen communities.

Tip: Expecting everyone to adapt to the common digital standard may not work for all employees within a company. Just as people like to drive in different lanes or learn via different tools and techniques, so is the case with Kaizen. A mix of physical and digital communication platform has proved most beneficial.

Tip: The Kaizen promotion office is the brain and limbs of Kaizen campaign. It is advisable to plan pre-event activities eight to nine weeks ahead, so they are completed in time.

The most basic way to get Kaizen rolling is by conducting a meeting and running the campaign like any other project ...

Step 2: Kaizen Project Management and Project Charter

Critical path method (CPM), Programs evaluation and review technique (PERT), Waterfall technique and RACI techniques have been used successfully to drive Kaizen projects. Personally, I prefer RACI. Most of the marketed project management software are good too. Hence, any project management tool one is comfortable with can be employed for Kaizen projects.

Agile Kaizen gives quick wins and promotes a positive impact to the Kaizen movement. It has been found that Kaizen project management tool combined with Agile facilitates rapid designing and prototyping, therefore is an excellent tool for drug discovery, product development, and scale-ups.

Regardless of the project management methodology employed careful consideration must be given to the overall project objectives, timelines, cost, as well as the roles & responsibilities of all participants and stakeholders. Kaizen project management function is an integral part of a company's governance board and oversees the creation, running of the Kaizen promotion office. Company's senior leadership team strategizes 'what' should happen based on the findings of value stream mapping. While the workforce design implementation strategies i.e. 'how' it will happen using Kaizen events.

Tip: Strategic Kaizen with Kanban framework reduces 'WIP' in manufacturing and distribution cycles and further helps to realize benefits of Kaizen campaign.

Kaizen Events

Kaizen events use the spirit of Kaizen to implement Kaizen principles and improvement ideas. Effective Kaizen event is well planned, well implemented, and well documented. Some events are suitable for project management, while some are aimed at local, operational, functional or departmental process improvements. Yet few others may have a cross-functional or even have companywide focus. The more challenging or widespread the Kaizen event's focus, the more planning, and communication will be needed for it to succeed.

A Kaizen event is a weeklong activity, usually pre-planned to have a start and close date. The campaign comprises training sessions on the first day, process walking and its analysis on day-2, followed by two days of ideation to seek improvement solutions for the problem process. On the final day, everyone is trained on the 'new' process, a report is prepared and presented to the group prior to wrap-up.

The events may sometimes run shorter for a half, 1 or 2 days. Shorter events have a narrow focus and usually work well after longer events, to achieve breakthroughs in selected areas. For example, starting 5S implementation in a department; creating visual controls in an area; reducing waste in a single area; rearranging layout of a small office etc. Shorter Kaizen events need less pre-event planning. While activities with wide focus or complex problems require more planning, communication to meet with success.

Kaizen events also bring forth enhanced job satisfaction as workers are engaged in more meaningful and collaborative work style with less stress. Moreover, when employees understand the 'why' behind 'what' is done, they build expertise around it, become good decision makers, and give enhanced performance and better productivity.

Kaizen Events Classification

Kaizen events could be classified based on their focus, frequency, and format of implementation. They may be periodic or just one-shot.

Various types of Kaizen event formats are- Kick-offs meetings, Project post-mortems, Development meetings, Customer feedback or Voice of customer (VOC) meetings, Design labs, Backlog pruning meetings, Root cause analysis, Off-site programs & strategy builders, Workouts or Kaizen Blitz- blitz meaning lightning in German; named because of the fast improvement that is attained through this format of event.

Kaizen events broadly include- training employees, process stapling, identifying process inefficiencies (muda), root cause analysis, finding improvement solutions, implementing changes, creating Kaizen reports, sustain improved process, communicate updates and sustain Kaizen culture within the company.

Step 3: Training

All employees must be trained about Kaizen process to bring about awareness as well as motivate employees towards the Kaizen movement.

Training Formats

Depending on the company's financial size, the number of employees, strength, budget, the number of physical locations, available technology and nature of the desired improvement, the preferred learning technique with a combination of different formats may be chosen.

Another important criterion determining training is employee's learning style. Various adult learning styles such as visual, kinesthetic, audible prevail. It is advisable to conduct a survey to evaluate employee learning style and their preferred method, prior to setting up the training program.

How can consultants help?

Most companies outsource training to external consultants. Various training formats available include- Gemba (worksite) training, online interactive training, teleseminars, webinars, conference room training, lunch-n-learn sessions, podcasts, books, voicemail training, email training, one-on-one mentoring.

Employees could subscribe to a course or update themselves via books or other learning tools. Companies usually reimburse full amount spent by the employee on training.

Step 4: Process Stapling

Process stapling is mapping out existing business process.

Let us consider an example- The process to be improved is to decrease number of days required to create a batch manufacturing document for a new capsule product. Several departments such as- planning, R&D, packaging, production, testing lab, quality, marketing, are involved in document making. Let us assume, it takes 30 days to finalize the document. Our objective is to shorten the time taken by a week, i.e. 30 days is the baseline and 21 days is the goal...

Process stapling involves creating a prop document and running it through each department and appropriate employees. The roles of these employees may be that of document writers, reviewers, approvers, issuers, users, signatories, auditors and record keepers. Every step the prop traverses is noted along with the time taken, number & type of problems faced en route, probable reasons for those problems, improvement suggestions etc.

Establishing baseline helps in identifying areas of inefficiencies; while collecting data via process stapling helps design new / improved process.

A companion tool to process stapling is benchmarking.

Benchmarking defines the comparison of a business or its process against others in terms of understanding where the business stands and how it can be advanced. It typically compares the practices used in one's business in comparison to others to find out the standards or practices which are most applicable. Benchmarking also shows the way business processes are approached, in what manner they're being done, how others are doing it, how current performance of a company measures against other organizations, and ways in which it can be improved.

Different types of benchmarking include the following-

- Process benchmarking.
- Financial benchmarking.
- Benchmarking from investor, public sector perspective.
- Performance benchmarking.
- Product benchmarking.
- Strategic benchmarking.
- Functional benchmarking.
- Operational benchmarking.
- Best-in-class benchmarking.

Benchmarking including process benchmarking, entails the development and learning involved by using comparisons as indicators, such as- quality, time, productivity, cost, profit and/or value. Benchmarking implementation can take a lot of time to set up since it requires a great deal of study of current practices.

Process benchmarking can be performed in increments or to the entire operations or a process. It is viewed as a tool for continuous improvement as opposed to a single event.

The reason why process benchmarking is vital to the success of a business is because, it clearly shows- where a business can make necessary changes, where there are the challenges, suggest new methods for improvement, and ways in which to make the business more efficient and effective.

The main types of process benchmarking include: internal, competitive, functional and generic benchmarking. Internal benchmarking compares one specific process in the organization to another company's method. Process benchmarking is the simplest form of benchmarking since it requires less research and implementation activity.

Competitive benchmarking refers to the comparison of a current process against main competitors (instead of the entire industry). This is viewed as the most challenging form of benchmarking due to the information that is required. Functional benchmarking uses the comparison against other organizations within the entire industry and general requires much less research than competitive benchmarking.

The information gathered through process of benchmarking can significantly advance a business and help to develop a greater advantage over competitors. It is also a good tool for motivating the company into a new and more successful direction, including bringing on Kaizen culture. Process benchmarking compares one's business against another's to find out what practices are obsolete and which should be used instead. There are several steps that make up a successful process benchmarking activity.

Different steps of Process Benchmarking

The first step in process benchmarking is to analyze and pinpoint the practices that are to be benchmarked. This can be done by finding out which practices have the largest impact on the organization's operations, governance, profits, shareholders, customers, budget, departments and so on. It is not necessary to undergo process benchmarking with the entire organization. Ideally, a company should be able to choose specific areas within the organization, which needs to be improved or changed. This stage can also be considered as the 'Identification stage'.

After the first stage of identification is complete, begins the next stage called as 'Planning stage'. It is much easier to come with a detailed outline that describes important aspects of the changes and how it will affect business processes. The next step is to find out the various processes that other organizations use. This is vital to make clear and valuable comparisons. Methods for finding out this information include research, conversations, interviews, surveys etc. Use this information to note the key differences between one's own and competitor organizations.

The third stage involves comparing one's organizational processes against those researched.

This requires detailed interpretation of gathered research, comparisons in written and diagrammatic form and other essential pieces of data. It will be easier to find out how performances compare when viewing the information this way.

The last stage out of the vital stages of process benchmarking is to make the necessary changes to the processes using different methodologies including Kaizen. There is no point in performing the previous stages if the changes are not going to be implemented, regardless of how drastic the change appears to be. It is necessary to come up with a plan of action to find out exactly how the changes will be implemented.

To increase the likelihood of success, it is vital for the employees to understand the reasons for change and that, the management must make sure that the employees are provided with the resources that are required to make the improvement.

Step 5: Conduct root cause analysis and future roadmaps

The first step is to choose where to conduct the first Kaizen event. At the start, choose an area that will have an impact but will not pose too many difficulties i.e. low hanging fruits.

Gain learnings from each event to make next event smoother to run successfully. Also, each new event provides a training ground for new joiners. As experience is gained, workforce gets more equipped and motivated to address complex issues.

Start slow and build momentum...

Let us revisit the Process Waste Scorecard. This is our primary reference for creating future action roadmaps. Conduct root cause analysis on each waste in the Process waste card, using Idea Analysis Cycle below-

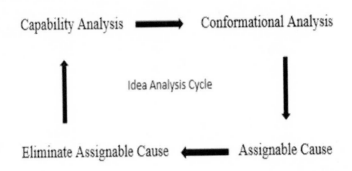

Generate ideas for improvement for each process and evaluate idea one at a time. Evaluate each improvement idea based on: (a) its potential benefit and (b) ease of implementation.

Potential benefit metric includes- quality, cost (ROI, top line, bottom line), delivery, safety, efficacy, employee morale, operational convenience, brand image, customer satisfaction, market share etc.

Ease of implementation metric includes-cost of working the idea, is the idea stand alone or in series or in sequence to another, degree of senior leadership & stakeholder support needed, idea complexity, time needed, competing priorities, technical difficulties, building management and HVAC system changes, dossier re-filings needed as per SUPAC, affected employee's resistance etc.

Tip: Add more metrics based on the type of process idea, the area of implementation, company size & work culture. A thorough evaluation of each idea is one of the guaranteed steps to success with Kaizen roll-out.

Assign each evaluated idea to appropriate quadrant of a Idea Management chart below based on its Potential benefits Vs Ease of implementation.

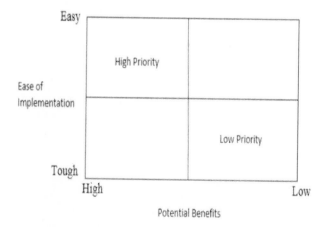

Ideas in each quadrant can be further rank-ordered using a prioritization matrix. Against each prioritized idea, write down the name(s) of who will do it? By when will they do it? How will they do it? Assign a team, design roles & responsibilities, and timelines for completion.

Create a schedule to initiate idea implementation. Communicate this information via all channels of Kaizen promotion office.

Step 6: Improve process

Traditionally, Kaizen process improvement kicks-off with 5S implementation. 5S workplace organization methodology implies a basis of improving an organization and is a vital aspect of creating an aesthetically pleasing workplace.

5S focuses largely on the aesthetic aspect of a business, which helps raise efficiency, safety, and simplicity. It can also be implemented in individual areas (such as certain open office areas, etc.) and differ between rooms, which allows it to be more lenient and appreciated by those that see the necessity of implementing it. Usually, managers oversee regulating and evaluating 5S functioning. This helps make it a more credible action and gain momentum as well.

Traditionally 5S methodology stands for five primary 5S phases: Sorting (in Japanese: **S**eiri), Streamlining workflow (in Japanese: **S**eiton), Systematic cleaning (in Japanese: **S**eiso),

Standardizing (in Japanese: **S**eiketsu) and Sustaining (in Japanese: **S**hitsuke). It was developed by *Hiroyuki Hirano*. However, the methodology is incorporated into the broader Kaizen methodology, which helps a company to improve continuously.

5S emphasizes organization, aesthetic order, standardization, and cleanliness. The reason that 5S is often used is because it has been found to raise efficiency, profitability, safety and service. Therefore, 5S may also be referred as a "Cycle of efficiency". It may seem like it is a given thing to incorporate these aspects into a business, but many fails to do so correctly. Implementing 5S allows the company to evaluate, monitor and change their company to suit these standards.

5S is commonly referred as- Sort, Set in Order, Shine, Standardize and Sustain.

Sort refers to a tagging system known as the 'Red Tag Technique'. Using this rule, those that are not sure of the use of an item are meant to move the item and discuss its necessity, or if not needed, get rid of it completely.

Set in Order refers to every item having its designated spot, therefore nothing is out of place and everything that is in place has a role.

Shine refers to monitoring and keeping areas clean via continuous, or frequent, cleaning and inspection.

Standardize means that the rules that have been implemented in hopes of keeping 5S working well are required to be followed.

Sustain refers to implementing 5S and the various techniques into a daily work schedule, thereby causing it to become habitual and stopping former disarray- habits from returning.

All kinds of businesses can benefit from using 5S methodology. It is most commonly found in the manufacturing industry sector but is also very popular amongst professional services, government offices, hospitals, office areas, libraries, hotels, warehouses, departmental stores, city premises, transportation and more.

For pharmaceuticals, 5S may not be directly applicable to the manufacturing areas since cGMP conditions are already present; but 5S can play a major role in other areas of a pharmaceutical, medical device and biotech companies. For example- Conference rooms benefit from using 5S since it helps contribute to the success of meetings. Other instances include, office areas especially shared offices, distribution channels, transportation and logistics, depots etc.

Advantages of 5S Workplace Organization Methodology

There are many advantages to using 5S at the workplace. One of the most important aspects of 5S is to get rid of items that are unnecessary, such as materials, supplies, and tools that are unused. This allows for greater efficiency by making it easier to find necessary items. It also encourages labeling, placing and organizing frequently used materials, tools and supplies to make them more accessible to users. In combination, these techniques result in less wasted time, in fact, allow time to be spent in a more productive manner.

Getting rid of unnecessary materials, equipment and tools as well as keeping areas clutter-free contribute to a lot more space. Space ends up costing money to a company and can be used in more beneficial ways once it is cleared. Whether it is the cost of heating, cooling, rental, cleaning or maintaining the area, when there is less junk, there is less money spent on maintenance and upkeep of the space.

Also, a clutter-free space makes it easier to prevent problems from occurring, or to take care of issues before they become even more problematic. This also contributes to the overall safety of a workplace.

Safety is a big issue that 5S addresses, by allowing clutter-free spaces to be monitored with ease. Having the necessary materials and tools saves time and improves efficiency, whilst lowering the risks of injury related to searching for these materials. A good example of this is a printer that is leaking. If there is a lot of clutter, it can be hard to notice that the ink is spilling or dripping, however, if the area is cleared, the leak can easily be noticed and fixed. Through standardization, practices that are deemed unsafe are not used. Employees can notice errors and make necessary changes.

Limitations of 5S Workplace Organization Methodology

While there are many benefits to implementing 55, it is good to be aware of its potential limitations as well. The most common problems when implementing 5S include, workplace problem misaddresses, struggles to change, deficiency of moral backing and misunderstanding the methodology itself.

It is not easy to create change in the workplace and 5S is known to cause large changes to occur. People get used to their way of things and routines, which can be difficult to change, especially if there is resistance to doing so. Therefore, it is necessary to introduce and implement 5S in increments, or at a slow pace, to allow people to get used to the idea of doing things in a different way. It is best to allow them to incorporate aspects of 5S into their daily habits without completely disrupting their norm in one go.

Another way to overcome this limitation is to introduce 5S methodology's concept during meetings and gauzing reaction. If the employees are interested in making the change, it will be that much easier to keep it going and to receive the necessary support.

The 5S methodology is also largely customizable and each company needs to find how it will benefit them in the best way. Therefore, it is not ideal to use a preexisting 5S plan from another company in hopes that it will reap the same results.

5S gets rid of unnecessary things in the workplace, but the framework that is used must be altered to suit each unique situation. Some workplaces may find that frequently used materials need to be brought closer to their areas, whereas others may need to clean out and reorganize their primary workspace.

5S has difficulty in excelling if it is not backed with the moral support of the management and employees alike, regardless of the type of organization or industry vertical. Management is required to monitor, evaluate and provide an example as to how 5S should work, as well as provide adequate staff and financial support.

Some organizations implement methodologies such as 5S and expect it to turn things around on its own. But this is impossible; 5S must be carefully implemented and monitored, even after success has been reached. It is also necessary to know exactly how 5S can benefit the company and not give it undue high hopes than it can fulfill.

Additional points to note during Kaizen Process Improvement Event include:

- Is Kaizen activity localized to a specific department or shall happen simultaneously companywide?
- SOP for Kaizen activities for multiple locations of organizations must be appropriately drafted and approved prior to implementation. Like other SOPs, Kaizen SOP is a live document.

- If the event must happen on the production floor, make sure cGMP conditions are never compromised. Take adequate precautions and maintain logs. Keep records of event start, end time, the team involved, equipment & area, product name with batch details, whether production was on-going or stopped for Kaizen to roll on.
- If production was stalled or stopped for Kaizen activity, appropriate line clearance procedure must be implemented before re-starting production. Special line clearance SOP must be created if need be. The SOP document must be approved as per established procedure and be 'live' before kicking-off Kaizen in that area.
- For any Kaizen activity where production or departmental activity needs to be stalled or stopped, a financial summary of expenses including cost of lost opportunity must be drafted and approved by finance head of the company, prior to rolling Kaizen in that department.

Things to watch out for-

- Manufacturing department may decline during Kaizen events. For example- production stoppages may be required to make significant changes in process or layout. A line might need to be shut down for extended time based on the changes being implemented or operators might need to be re-trained to work the new process.

Plan advance production to cover for such eventualities.

- It is not enough that the person leading the event understands Kaizen. Everyone must be trained. Usually, external consultants are hired as Kaizen coach. Make sure consultants don't impose their ideas on your company's workforce. Worker participation is the key. Consultants must involve workforce to ring in process improvement solutions.

Tip: Complete maximum of process improvement activity within scheduled time of Kaizen event. What couldn't be achieved must be noted on a follow-up sheet and completed quickly via a short Kaizen event.

Take-a-Five

Take five minutes to think and jot down answers for-

- Would you like to add any rules to the above list?
- Calculate and record the cycle time of key business processes in your company.

Kaizen Event Implementation Quick Reference List

The Kaizen promotion office initiates following activities-

Pre-event:

- Create Kaizen Charter form, Checklist and facilitate the practice of Kaizen methodology.
- Get approval from the sponsor.
- Schedule Kaizen event dates. Notify all staff about the event (open-door policy).
- Report Kaizen metrics, process data statistics and communicate within the organization via Kaizen Newspaper.
- Gather supplies (viz. Easel, self-sticking easel paper, post-its, markers, camera, computer) the day before the Event.

Day 1:

- Review of Kaizen Elements, Rules, Tools.

- Warm-up Activities (The Customer, 5-Whys).

- Develop Current State Map (take photos).

- Identify Value-Added (VA), Non-Value-Added (NVA), and Non-Value-Added but Required activities (NVR).

- Calculate VA, NVA, NVR, Takt time and Total cycle time of process to be improved.

Day 2:

- Identify 'waste' / inefficiency in the existing process.

- Create Future State Map (take photos). Select processes for re-design.

  Tip: Idea Management chart data will be handy here.

- Develop Standard Work and Single Piece Flow.

- Develop Visual Workplace.

Day 3:

- Determine if all 'goals' have been met.

- Identify outcomes (performance measures).

- Complete Kaizen Implementation Plan (limit to two weeks).

- Closing: Create report- Lessons learned, future items to address.

- Take team photo.

Post Event:

- Present report to upper management.

- Develop Kaizen standardized work and continue staff training.

- Work Kaizen Implementation Plan and track results.

- Celebrate and communicate success with others via Kaizen Newspaper.

- Coordinate rewards and recognition.

Checklist to be periodically reviewed:

✓ Did everyone get involved understand and agree about the project direction & objectives?

✓ Did we have the appropriate skills in the project?

✓ Did we have and use appropriate tools and techniques?

✓ Did entire team work well together?

✓ Were our stakeholders kept up-to-date on the project programs?

✓ Did we manage project challenges effectively?

✓ Did we encourage and deal with feedback effectively?

✓ Did we anticipate project problems effectively?

✓ Were agreed procedures followed as planned?

✓ What is the accuracy of progress measured?

✓ EVM (earned value measurement) i.e. Cost Vs Schedule.

✓ Are we doing appropriate forecasting and sourcing early warranties?

✓ Did we follow project structure?

✓ Did we plan for 'unknowns' appropriately?

✓ Gap analysis (Plan Vs Fact) and scope control.

✓ Are we guiding people after each change? Coordinating AAR (After Action Reviews) process?

✓ Are we dealing with resistance to change? The change curve.

Thought Leader Insights

A few years ago, I was leading business turnaround campaign in a pharmaceutical contract research company's R&D division. Our goals were to shorten product development timelines and get existing clients to give us repeat business to the tune of $35M USD.

At the outset, we initiated baselining to understand ground realities. The next step was to strategize campaign roadmaps. We found that the situation was deplorable. All projects were running late by 25-30 months! Some of them were four or more years overdue, many products had quality issues, clients were fuming (understandably so).

To my utter horror, in many instances, I noticed huge numbers of experimental batches (as many as 100 to 400) were conducted, yet there was no sight of a stable ready product. I wondered what was going on- why does a seemingly simple looking generic tablet or capsule product takes 250 experiments for formulating it. As if this wasn't enough, the product fails at two months stability test! If you have ever been in a similar situation as I was then, I am sure you will resonate with me.

After 9 months of strategic working and resource re-allocations, we brought about a turnaround. All stuck-up projects were completed. Customer relationship management was at its premium best and we succeeded in ringing in $40 M of repeat business (Vs $35 million business target).

*How did this turnaround happen in
just 9 months?*

Let me share my secret, we practiced Kaizen every minute of the day.

Further, research and manufacturing focussed Kaizen implementation enabled the organization to unlock talents and abilities of the workforce, allowing decisions to be made by people closest to the work-process, despite being lowest on the corporate ladder. Senior leadership limited to simply giving directions. This freed them from day-to-day micro-management and allowed them to focus on earning revenues, performance analytics, removing operational hurdles and facilitate employee development.

Kaizen approach allowed problems to be solved quickly, everyone was learning by doing and working together to deliver sustainable results consistently.

"As a practicing Continuous Improvement consultant over the years, I have witnessed several organizations who believe they are 'in Kaizen' all the time, even though their profits show otherwise. It helps to have an Expert conduct comprehensive review of current processes and techniques to ensure they are optimally sequenced for maximum benefits."

- Dr. Shruti U. Bhat

Here are few attributes of properly run Kaizen event-

- Value stream driven.
- Total employee workforce involvement.
- Cross-functional teamwork.
- Smart and aggressive goal- driven.
- Undivided focus on achieving goals.
- Short duration of 5- 7 days.
- Mudas (wastes) minimized or eliminated.
- Rapid decisions and stakeholder buy-ins.
- One-hundred percent thorough implementation of proposed changes.
- Changed process training.
- New process sustainability built-in- by-design.

- Employee overall training, development and morale building.
- Leaders become mentors eventually.

What can't be done by advice can often be done by example - Unknown

---

Coming up in the next chapter, we will consider few real-life case studies and examples from pharmaceutical, medical device, and biotech companies worldwide ...

Chapter 7: Examples and case studies

In this chapter, we will see ...

- ✓ Kaizen for Drug-Device Shop Floor Productivity Improvement.
- ✓ Kaizen for Vendor Management.
- ✓ Kaizen for New Product Scale-up and Technology Transfer.
- ✓ Kaizen for Packaging and Product Anti-Counterfeiting.
- ✓ Kaizen for Designing Pharmaceutical Facility Layouts.
- ✓ Kaizen for Business Development.
- ✓ Kaizen for Pharmaceutical Innovations.

Shruti Bhat

I was talking with one of the employees from a Healthcare center in Canada about her thoughts on 'Continuous Improvement'. She not only shared with me her views but also introduced me to 70 colleagues within her organization, so they could share their views with me. I learned that they staunchly believe senior management often link 'Continuous Improvement' programs as a mask to cut jobs.

As a Kaizen and Lean Six Sigma Consultant, I have often heard such views. But what appalled me was that, this organization had initiated 'Continuous Improvement' campaigns twice with meager success and didn't do a thorough investigation of failures!

A point I sincerely insist during my talks with companies that come to me for consultation, is that communication with employees must be precise, clear and honest, so they participate with focus, vigor, and confidence. Creating and bringing about a change is a mammoth task by itself. Larger the organization and diverse the workforce, bigger is the challenge."

Presented here are few examples and case studies of Kaizen applied in pharmaceuticals, medical device and biotech companies in US, Canada, India, Brazil, UK, Switzerland, Netherlands and GCC countries. In compliance to confidentiality clauses, details about company and brand names have not been disclosed.

Kaizen for Improving Shop Floor Productivity (Shop floor management via Kaizen with Jidoka, Poka-Yoke, Just-in-time and CAPA)

This Example pertains to Kaizen event in improving shop floor operations (excluding facility design change).

Step 1: Kick-off Kaizen on the shop floor with 5S implementation on shop floor operations procedures. Set up three Kaizen sub-teams.

Step 2: Head to creating workflow design. Workflow design finds out several solutions to specific problems and makes it easier to find out which solution is the best for implementation. Control-flow, resources, material handling and data handling workflows are most frequently created. These advanced tools usually are combined with Kaizen to speed-up Kaizen events and bring on change quicker. To begin with, a workflow sketch was created by adding modules and providing the appropriate information for various sub-processes.

Step 3: Using the process workflow sketch, SIPOC and Activity diagrams were done to understand types, levels, and employees involved in process inputs and outputs. The process inefficiencies were identified, a process waste card created, extent and cost of waste estimated, improvement ideas generated, a waste/inefficiency elimination strategic plan was designed and a Kaizen campaign for its implementation was developed.

Step 4: The Kaizen campaign which also included Kaizen events were successfully conducted. Since Kaizen, the new 'improved' process proactively led to products with zero defects, facility with zero accidents, zero equipment breakdowns, and zero injuries.

Some additional precautions taken during the Kaizen campaign were:

- Made sure cGMP conditions were never compromised. Took adequate precautions and maintained logs. Records of event start, end time, the team involved, equipment & area, product name with batch details were maintained.

- SOPs for Kaizen activities for multiple locations of organizations were appropriately drafted and approved prior to implementation.

- Whenever production was expected to be stalled or stopped for Kaizen activity, appropriate line clearance procedure was implemented before re-starting production. In instances where financial implications of stopping production was not readily available, the data was generated impromptu; a financial summary of expenses including cost of lost opportunity, was drafted and approved by finance head of the company, prior to rolling Kaizen in that area.

Tip: Introducing total productive maintenance (TPM) in Kaizen events at shop floor further improves equipment maintenance, so there will be no breakdowns, defects, and accidents. While maximizing overall equipment efficiency (OEE), Kaizen-TPM created a shared responsibility between the operators and maintenance personnel, empowered operators to actively maintain the equipment they use.

Kaizen event results dashboard:

- ✓ Tablet manufacturing facility: reduced throughput time by 70%.
- ✓ Packaging line for solid orals: Increased output by 36%
- ✓ Pharmaceutical contract manufacturing site: reduced changeover time by 80%
- ✓ Inventory levels: reduced by 20 to 70%
- ✓ Equipment uptime enhanced by 90 %
- ✓ Number of conflict management incidences at the shop floor dropped significantly since Kaizen campaign.

Kaizen- Jidoka- Kaizen also enhances workforce morale more so in production areas. Japanese call 'Jidoka' referring to the capability of stopping production line if a problem should occur.

Jidoka is an important pillar in Toyota Production Systems (TPS) and simulates the concept of 'Zero defect'. Jidoka works excellent for batch processes and requires each worker on the production line to be vigilant for defective parts. Under Jidoka philosophy, each batch operation of the production process is driven by a different group of workers. Thus, each worker group acts

228

as a pseudo-customer, and checks all items coming to their group for working the production process. Jidoka philosophy complements a company's zero defect quality policy.

The main stages of Jidoka are to notice a problem, stop production, solve the problem, evaluate and correct the reason due to which problem occurred in the first place regardless of whether machines or humans are involved. Control charts, Check sheets, Pareto charts and Ishikawa diagrams are usually employed in the decision making.

Kaizen-Jidoka is a great way to stop defect-ridden products from ending up with the customers.

Although, Jidoka originated in Japanese auto industry, if applied correctly on the pharmaceutical, medical device and biotech company shop floors, Jidoka will help minimize both alfa and beta sampling errors, bring huge savings in IPQC testing costs, and reduce production overheads.

Kaizen-Jidoka is very effective in bottle packaging departments. Kaizen- Jidoka also minimizes chances of equipment malfunctions. Kaizen- Jidoka works excellent for all production lines, however, best suited for semi-automated manufacturing lines.

A major cause of decreased shop floor productivity is accidents. Safety breaches lead to more accidents. Safety training is not good enough. The facility must be designed and geared up always to prevent mishaps. *A vital tool for this is* **Kaizen-Poka-Yoke**.

Poka-Yoke is commonly referred to as 'error proofing or mistake-proofing'. The process of Poka-Yoke is to observe processes and catch mistakes before they happen and/or get transitioned or escalated to the next level.

Some of the pharmaceutical processes have traditionally employed mistake-proofing for example, 100% inspection of eye drop or injection vials against black/white background, 100% inspection of tablet strips or blister packs for blank pockets etc.

Applying Poka-Yoke at each production process produces enormous benefits.

Kaizen event results dashboard:

Conducting Kaizen events to implement Poka- Yoke has minimized safety incidences in bulk drug manufacturing and biotech reactors by as much as 90% and improved productivity by 250%.

Kaizen with Just-in-time (JIT) improves production efficiency- Just-in-time production strategy hastens return on investment (ROI) by reducing inventory, wastes associated with carrying costs, by obtaining goods only when they are required in the production process. This drastically lowers cost of inventory. It requires the producer's foresight into accurately predicting what, when and how much or how many raw material items will be required.

When Toyota started to use JIT, they figured out that, if they evaluate where the purchasing flaws were, they could end up building cars at a faster pace and at minimum cost. This fostered their idea of having cars that were built-to-order, so there would be no potential loss if the car did not sell. JIT eliminated risk entirely.

Toyota experts also found that they could rely on certain suppliers instead of multiple ones. Further, the suppliers were advised to provide only those materials which matched specifications. This positively influenced material receipts bearing consistent quality. Also, it significantly reduced the need for raw material quality checks, as well as inventory build-up.

Storage costs can be a significant drawback for companies. JIT allows companies to store materials as needed. This facilitates better cash flow and lowers amount of goods held in stock and storage space. The freed-up space can be used for something more productive, while the savings generated due to low stocked up inventory could be used elsewhere viz. R&D, marketing, facility upgrades, training etc.

JIT strategy also allows companies to gain an advantage over their competition because it creates a business that is flexible and sees the need for effective communication between suppliers and customers. Moreover, JIT permits companies to make quick decisions in response to the demands of the market.

Although pharmaceutical business operations are different from the auto companies, experience gained with JIT implementation in the auto sector could be transferred straight-up into life sciences business or, for that matter any industry vertical.

Kaizen event results dashboard:

Kaizen events for identifying flaws in material procurement and logistics department within a pharmaceutical company has saved over $ 400,000 the first year and similar amounts year-on-year. Introducing JIT further enhances savings by 70%.

Tip: For pharmaceuticals, excipient details, raw material quality profile, specification, and vendor information get recorded rather locked into the CMC part of a product's dossier. This must encourage JIT. Despite the benefits, most pharmaceutical companies don't use JIT, save not using it to its fullest potential!

Tip: JIT does require investment in planning and good Information Technology (IT) services. Currently, most companies implement ERP systems, hence introducing JIT in such IT savvy companies becomes easy; although the presence of ERP system is not a necessity for JIT to roll-in. JIT philosophy works excellent in non-ERP based organizations too if their IT systems allow good communication between the company and its vendors, to manage orders and production planning details. Also, appropriate risk control mechanisms must be in place.

Kaizen with CAPA- Corrective Action and Preventive Action, also known as CAPA, is an improvement measure to organization's business and/or technical processes. CAPA as the name suggests has two components-

1. Corrective Actions i.e. once a problem is known, its root cause is identified and appropriate corrective action is put in place.
2. Preventive Actions, are actions to be put in place to stop problems/ mishaps from occurring or reoccurring and aim to anticipate potential issues before they occur.

There are paper and electronic versions of CAPA processes. CAPA has three stages:

Stage 1: To identify and document the reason for a problem's occurrence.

Stage 2: The entire system's processes are reviewed to confirm that such and /or similar problems will not occur in the future.

Stage 3: The effect of the problem is analyzed and its impact on the company's product or service is estimated.

Preventive action processes involve taking necessary actions to guarantee that an error will not occur or recur. It is often necessary to have an analysis performed of the system and its processes, which will help determine the requirements for changes involved so that the problem does not occur. Preventive actions require a set program of activities that allow for change to be implemented and monitored.

The USFDA considers the CAPA system as a 'single' system. As per FDA's latest updates, eight features are essential in a company's CAPA system:

1. Thorough investigation of the matter.

2. Investigation – a determination of the root cause(s).

3. What corrective actions have been taken to fix the issue. What preventive actions will be taken to avoid the issue from recurring.

4. Verification and re-qualification of the redesigned process.

Tip: Business process validation helps to determine whether the changes are effective and if the business process should continue to be used. Business process qualification implies actions required to verify that the processes does what it purports to do.

Problems that arise during one or more of stages of a business's workflow, can lead to major disruption thus such as- inability to continue producing goods, order demands, shipping orders, defective products reaching market place etc. These side effects can greatly affect customer satisfaction, company's reputation and revenue. Business process qualification helps find product or process defects and minimizes its negative impact on the business's overall performance.

While undergoing business process qualification, the processes are monitored and evaluated at each stage. If any problems or issues were to arise, the information is immediately distributed to the appropriate department and process scheduled for repair.

Business process qualifications are performed at different stages of a process, such as- project, periodic or continuous basis and can be done via manually or automated using software to track data gather.

5. Change process to be installed.

6. Communicating the change to all stakeholders.

7. Management review of the situation.

8. Document everything – provide an 'audit trail' of sequence of activities.

Tip: Effective business processes increase customer satisfaction and value. A successful way to increase business process effectiveness is to add greater focus on daily business activities and figure out how they can be made more effective and efficient.

Traditionally business operations have focussed on 5Ms- men (and women), machines, methods, materials and money. With transiting century, a paradigm shift occurred- Time and Technology got added to the original 5M concept. 21stC businesses work on 5M +2T. In fact, technology relates to men, machines, and materials as its subsets.

Kaizen events (1-2 days campaign) shorten CAPA process and helped enhance shop floor productivity.

Kaizen event results dashboard:

As much as 7% productivity improvement was achieved by using Kaizen with CAPA for fully automated lines within pharmaceutical, medical device and biotech companies. Manual and semi-automated lines showed 12-15 % productivity rise.

The productivity rise is measured using productivity quotient:

Productivity quotient= <u>Drug units produced</u>
Number of FTE

(Note: FTE, Full Time Employee).

The concept of productivity quotient can, however, be employed in all areas of pharmaceutical business and not just shop floor. Identifying opportunity is a pro-active approach Vs solving problems, which is a reactive approach. Worst is not knowing that a problem exists!

*"We have always done it this way".
Isn't that a familiar statement, we
tend to hear? Just because something
is traditionally done, doesn't make it
right, does it?*

Improving productivity within tablet department-

A few years ago, I had a mammoth task of improving productivity of tablet coating department of a pharmaceutical company. This was a growing company, small but with extremely rigid work culture, and not many technical experts within the company. Just one guy, who thought he knew it all and everyone followed blind-folded. The senior management wanted to bring radical changes in their business and didn't now how, so they approached me.

"What should we do?" they asked.

My response was- "Either hire people who are job-trained or train your employees on topics that are directly relevant to their line of work. Everyone associated with tablet coating needs to take a refresher in coating technologies. These trainings are provided free-of-cost by several companies selling ready-to-coat materials. Then carry out Kaizen Blitz events to address your specific problem. The ideation arising out of Blitz event will pave way for improvement strategies".

Kaizen event results dashboard:

Technical as well as Kaizen training boot camps were conducted. Effective change management style was enforced to create Kaizen culture and implement Kaizen campaigns. After seven months of consistent Kaizen efforts, the first signs of success were realized- Productivity improved by 30%, wastes reduced by 50% and employee absenteeism reduced by 25%.

The largest room in the world is the room for Improvement - Unknown

Kaizen for Vendor Management

Kaizen is useful for vendor development as well...

Relationship management with vendors is a critical task for business leaders. Invite vendors to your Kaizen Blitz campaigns. Their suggestions help you to improve your internal processes and speed deliverables. Also, your suggestions can help a vendor improve their logistics or many a times even their product.

Kaizen event results dashboard:

Kaizen campaigns held in our organization helped our vendor to develop a new design of extruder- marumerizer machine. As a thank you, he gave us 90% discount on the purchase of the equipment; a win-win!

30% of company's overheads were saved after Kaizen Blitz campaign for procurement processes.

The new procurement process included vendor rating points to be given to a vendor for his overall performance for all the items that vendor supplies, optimally it is based on individual items of supply. A vendor's performance is rated and compared with other vendors supplying the same or similar kind of items. Bring in competition in price negotiations, spread risk of non-availability or shortages over several suppliers.

Example-

7 Points weightage criteria:

25 % Delivery (On time as per order)
05 % Quantity (matching order)
30 % Quality (matching specifications)
15 % Bid Price (prices lowest amongst bidders)
05 % Low Price (lowest in the market)
15 % Capability to meet emergency orders
05 % Good track record of material supply to the company

In past six months, a vendor has:
- Delivered 'on time' & 'as per order' 14 out of 20 times
- 3% rejects
- Failed capability of emergency delivery 5% of time
- Delivered at a price of $110 Vs $100 average bid price.
- Delivered at a price of $110 Vs $95 lowest in market.

Rating:
$0.25 \times 14/20 \times 100 = 17.5$ points for delivery
$0.05 \times 14/20 \times 100 = 3.5$ points for quantity
$0.3 \times 97/100 \times 100 = 29.1$ points for quality
$0.15 \times 100/110 \times 100 = 13.6$ points for bid price
$0.05 \times 95/110 \times 100 = 4.32$ points for low price
$0.15 \times 95/100 \times 100 = 14.25$ points for emergency supply capability

0.05 x 95/100 x 100 = 4.75 points for good supply track record

Total rating = 87.02 points

Tip: Over long periods of relationship building, the vendor can be pooled into 'JIT' pipeline thus, giving advantage of low inventories, more profits margins, low working capital blocks, therefore better cash-flow management.

A few years ago, my team revived a sick contract research company using JIT, where the entire formulation R&D for over two years, was operated using 'samples' from vendors; resulting in direct savings of 30% in R&D budget!

Other processes improved using Kaizen events were-

- Selection of material and its movement from the supply source to the manufacturing facility and making the product available to the customer at the right place, time etc.

- Selection of warehouse location.

- Route scheduling.

- Depots/ supply centers.

- Transport modes.

As decisions about logistics have their effect on inventories, packaging, material handling, purchasing, marketing (and sales) divisions and vice versa; Kaizen teams, in this case, were cross-functional comprising of R&D, logistics, manufacturing, vendors, transport providers, labors etc.- *a classic combination of* **Kaizen with Keiretsu**.

Tip: Japanese Keiretsu i.e. a group of business establishments come together to do business together and reap rewards. The buyer will try to find out the reasons for the higher costs of the supplier and then suggest ways of controlling it. Teamwork rewards are also passed on to the customers as they consistently get good quality and lower prices.

Kaizen for Scale-up and Technology Transfer

One of my clients wanted to construct a state-of-the-art USFDA compliant facility by breaking down their existing plant. This meant that 55 products manufactured in that facility must get transferred to another site. A gap analysis, tech-transfer protocols and detailed project plan were done.

We realized that this mammoth task would need a year to complete! Blitz Kaizen was used to identify risks, prioritize action items.

Kaizen -Doing the rights things right!

Technology transfer from R&D to pilot plant and/or commercial manufacturing is a complex process, especially because of the product/ process's newness, technology, launch deadlines etc. The focus

241

of the entire organization shifts to the R&D tech-transfer expert.

Creation of new product batch card is the first step of the tech-transfer process, which is complex enough, doesn't have to be long –drawn. A 3-day short Kaizen event was scheduled to identify inefficiencies in decision-making process for finalizing production date.

Kaizen event results dashboard:

Pre-Kaizen, creating a batch card took 30 days Vs 17 days post-Kaizen.

Set up Kaizen sub-team, involving the R&D scientist/ design engineer, Tech-transfer officer, Tech-transfer manager, Production supervisor, Production planner, Purchase Head, Analytical chemist and seven operators who would be involved in the manufacturing and testing of the new product.

The team kicked-off Kaizen by improving information needed for the issue of a bill of material, spare parts control, and implementation of the 5S on existing technology transfer standard operating procedures.

The Kaizen event also identified metrics for proposed process improvement.

Tip: Business process improvement metrics are tools used to analyze, monitor and enhance the performances performed within an organization. One of the best tools for using metrics to measure business process improvement is business intelligence software.

Change Management incorporates metrics into business process improvement and allows organizations to follow the path of various activities that relate to alterations. This method requires different sets of data regarding change and data, which is collected, joined and concluded to measure the benefits. It makes the requirements of data clear and concise to view.

Metrics must be compared against business goals to be meaningful. Metrics in business are only applicable in the right context. While a large sum of money in sales might seem like a lot to an average reader, when compared with the company's earning goals, the sales amount might indicate that the company is just managing to keep its head above waters!

Another important stage in tech-transfer is decision making as to when to commence first production batch or whether to produce in-house or outsource. Larger the organization, longer is the time for decision making and elaborate the process.

In this case study, the company's existing scale-up process needed meeting attendance of 31 members, who used up 15 business days to finalize a production date!

Existing meeting team members (A) include-
Design scientist, Lab Head, Analytical chemist,
Development Head, Procurement Manager,
Manufacturing Head, QA Head, QA Manager,
Warehouse Manager, Marketing team, R&D team
and Project Managers; altogether 31 people attend
the meeting.

Key process input-

1. Bill of materials describing raw material
   and pack material quantities along with
   compliance specifications, test methods
   and timelines for material deliveries.
2. Manufacturing batch cards for scale-up of
   the new product from lab to production
   site.

Key process output-

1. To arrive at a decision whether product
   manufacturing shall be done in-house or
   outsourced.
2. Number of scale-up batches to be taken
   (depended on the complexity of product
   technology).
3. To create a list of potential challenges to be
   faced at production site during scale-up
   operation.

To improve-

1. Decrease members attending from existing
   31 to 9. Only members close to the process
   shall attend the meeting; everyone else to
   receive minutes of meeting for information.
   The new list of attendees (B) would include-
   Design scientist, Lab Head, Analytical

chemist, Procurement Manager, Manufacturing Supervisor, QA Manager, Production planner, one member from the marketing team and Project Leader.
2. Number of days to achieve key process output to be reduced.

Change process:

Set up a sub-team, headed by Kaizen champion to study the existing process via process stapling. They also interviewed several employees in various departments such as R&D, manufacturing, testing lab, quality, packaging, business development etc.

A Kaizen event was scheduled to generate process improvement ideas.

Brainstorming, SIPOC, Arrow diagrams, Decision trees and other tools were employed. The proposed 'improvement' workflow was communicated to all stakeholders for their suggestions/ recommendations and later finalized.

A likely question will occur to most- why have a 'elaborate' Kaizen event to make a simple change such as this one? The answer is two folds- first, because- Kaizen works best by making simple changes to simple as well as complex problems. Secondly, such instances although seem simple at the surface, aren't really so. The reason being, when people are involved, there is so much spoken as well as unspoken talk, sentiments, behaviors and attitudes. Such seemingly simple changes if not brought about in a methodical way, can lead to persistent conflicts, demotivation, employee turnover etc. In extreme cases, such matters can bring a huge set back to the entire year's performance of the company.

Kaizen event results dashboard:

The improved process needed only 9 meeting attendees (instead of 31) and 5 meeting hours (instead of previous 8 hours) thereby freeing more number of employee hours for constructive work. The improved process helped production date to be finalized in 13 days Vs 15 days via old process. Further, the Kaizen event generated 14 % savings in company's overhead costs in the first year followed by 9% savings year on year, till date.

Note: Details of this case study including process maps are available for free review at my blog-

http://www.drshrutibhat.com/blog/case-study-improving-scale-up-and-tech-transfer-processes-via-kaizen

Kaizen for Pharmaceutical Packaging and Product Anti- Counterfeiting

A significant advantage of Kaizen is that it can be used to solve minutest of problems and still give fantastic results.

Here is another study-

A pharmaceutical major in eye formulations with over 75% market share in ophthalmic business decided to introduce eye drops in automated liquid packaging (ALP) vials instead of traditional glass vials. ALP was found to be cost-effective and prevented product counterfeiting. Also, eye drops in ALP were marketed in both single and multi-dose bottles. These saved dollars for the patients as they now had an option to buy small doses as necessary; an unmet need.

Patient acceptance of clear eye drops in ALP was great. Obviously, they expected similar results with suspension eye drops. To their dismay, huge complaints poured in claiming the product was allegedly non-efficacious. The claim was absurd, as there was no change done to the formulation, processing or quality standards. It was a simple case of change of primary pack i.e. formulation that was filled in glass vials was now being offered in ALP vials (both single and multi-dose).

As expected there was a huge uproar. Finance and sales departments projected humongous losses; that added to the stress of all R&D and manufacturing personnel. If you are a tech-transfer scientist, you can easily visualize the scenario and gravity of the matter!

To begin with, all production batch cards, process conditions, in-process testing, end-product testing, drug content, stability, extractability and dose uniformity data were checked. Control samples were studied.

Everything was found to be perfectly in order. So, what was going wrong? Why was the product acting up non-efficacious?

With a crisis on hand, suggestions started pouring into R&D wings from all directions. Some suggested product re-formulation, few recommended transitioning product back to glass vials, while others voiced negative opinions. The R&D and Ops team were surrounded by chaos, confusion, rising tempers, slowing sales and growing inventories of product returns. And, I was brought in as a Consulting SME (Subject Matter Expert).

As a Kaizen & Lean Six Sigma consultant over a decade, the first thing I said was- "a crisis scene needs utmost self-restraint by all heads of department; their degree of self-restraint will alleviate employee insecurities, fears and thus propel them to ideate 'right things' and to set 'right things right' quicker than one can possibly imagine.

Typically, we witness everyone getting into investigating 'who' made the mistake rather than 'what' made the mistake to happen. Never blame people, but the process. Once the problem process is identified, it can not only be corrected but also prevented from a relapse".

Coming back to the project at hand, after collecting feedback from everyone, I recommended that the company initiate a Kaizen Blitz campaign with an objective to investigate deeper and ideate future course of action based on 'bare' facts and not on 'hearsay'.

At the Blitz campaign, we uncovered two important points:

1. All suspension products in ALP did not indicate 'non-efficacy' complaints.

2. The problem was exhibited by products containing 'white' drug. Eye drops containing off-white or colored drug(s) showed no complaints.

The Kaizen team conducted a brainstorming session. We concluded that the label dimension on the ALP vials must be reduced by few millimeters. This will allow patients to notice the white drug sediment and shake the product well, before use. The change was implemented on a pilot scale and viola- no complaints!

Kaizen event results dashboard:

Kaizen Blitz campaign provided the company, with most cost-effective and practical solution to the problem, in just seven days.

Kaizen is the shortest-cut to a successful product and/or process improvement venture!

Kaizen for Designing Facility Layouts

A few years ago, a pharmaceutical giant was designing a $60 million global research park. The state-of-the-art facility was projected to design and develop solid oral dosage forms for global markets. Budgets were forecasted and sanctioned. One year down the line, members of management board changed. New office bearers decided to widen project scope without enhancing budgeted dollars! Doesn't this happen all the time- Aren't we expected to do more with less?

Well, in this case the scope change was-more number of products in the development pipeline consequently more stability samples; thus, higher number of stability study chambers and more floor space would be needed to house them. And, all of this to be achieved within previously sanctioned budget and facility layout!

Two Kaizen Blitz events were run to find effective solutions to this problem-

Kaizen Blitz Event-1 was run for evaluating facility design layouts, potential batch sizes, counts of stability samples, stability study inventory loads and warehousing schematics. The material handling cost between 2 work areas (departments) is the product of the distance between the 2 work areas and the number of loads that are handled between the 2 departments during a unit period. The sum of the product for all the combinations of departments should be minimum for an optimal plant layout. This can be expressed as:

Minimize $\sum_{iy}$ diy x Liy

diy = distance between departments i and y

Liy = number of loads/ time moved between I and y

Therefore, to design plant by process layout is to gather load summary.

Through Gemba walks on facility blueprint, potential operational flaws (based on production process technology) were identified- extended changeover times, too long downtimes and a lack of internal flow within the factory and to optimize load balance. To solve these problems, it was planned to implement Daily Kaizen, followed by SMED, as Daily Kaizen meetings supported better teamwork.

Kaizen Blitz Event-2 was run to generate ideas about how to do sampling and place samples on stability (complying to ICH recommendations).

Kaizen event results dashboard:

Improved stability chamber capacity utilization by 27%.

Together Kaizen events 1 and 2 resulted in net savings of $10 million, which was 16.7% of budgeted cost!

Kaizen for Business Development

Kaizen Blitz is useful not only in R&D, Ops and quality departments, but also, in non-technical areas of life sciences companies. Let me quote an incident-

At monthly board meeting of a pharmaceutical contract research and development company's Business Development Head stated "We are losing potential clients because we are unable to bid within allotted time"

This company is on my clientele for several years. I recommended that they run a Kaizen Blitz campaign. Until then, the company had never tried Kaizen within business development (BD) division.

Process stapling indicated- BD forwards bid-proposal in 23 days Vs call of 15 days. It receives reports from different departments viz. project manager, R&D, Patents, Testing lab, Ops, and QA. BD then compiles information to create the bid proposal.

The Kaizen event revealed a multitude of root causes for the problem. At the end of the Kaizen event, it was decided that various departments will not generate reports- that's straight two mudas down- Waiting, Excess documentation!

Based on the bid features, BD will create bid proposal template and upload it to the company's Cloud-based server, permitting all departments to access information and update bid template document simultaneously.

The Patents team will review applicable patents, provide a summary of claims and potential ways of circumventing enforced patents. The R&D team would highlight formulation challenges, assign development times and costs. Ops, QA, and testing lab will input their part of the offering directly into the above template.

Since the document is stored on Cloud-server, everyone would get to view and update bid data file simultaneously. Information will be simply inputted into the document template (Vs typing & compiling reports). Also, there is no scope for documents to go back and forth, therefore, there will be neither rework nor delay.

Further, the Cloud-based automation immediately tracked the source of 'slow input' thus, no blame game. The process is transparent and all teams could receive a status update automatically by opting for electronic notifications.

Kaizen event results dashboard:

The improved process readied bid-proposals within 10 business days Vs 23 days by old process.

Kaizen for Pharmaceutical Innovations and Clinical Research

You cannot develop an electric bulb by continuous improvement of candles

Kaizen is very effective for incremental improvements or daily makeover, to improve productivity without any or significant capital inputs or hiring. Up to 30% cost can be saved at scale-up and tech-transfer stages using Kaizen in R&D and manufacturing Ops departments.

When I talk with heads life sciences organizations, a common challenge they seem to face, is to translate ideas into profits. Also, I notice a 'generic' outlook about innovation, which is- Innovation is everybody's business. My view here is – That's true ONLY for those doing incremental innovations such as cost-effective production, cheaper logistics, continuous improvement etc.

Kaizen helps companies in conducting such incremental innovation in a big way, A point to note is that, innovation is a full-time job and can't be done on a part-time basis. Also, skills set needed for innovation is different from those required to run a company's existing product development department. If your R&D head has multiple roles to play that is running the development lab as well as build innovation, this means your innovation mission is sure to fail!

While 'Breakthrough innovations' CAN'T be everyone's business. Organizations, right at the outset, need to have complete clarity about the path they wish to take regarding innovation.

For path-breaking innovations to be a reality, there must be a committed 'Innovation' leader with a dedicated taskforce and allotted finances.

Another significant element of succeeding with Innovation is the effective handling of 'Innovation killers'.

Tip: Kaizen events can be used to handle Innovation killers, here's how to–

- ✓ Demonstrate the damage they cause.
- ✓ Stop excuses and limit criticism.
- ✓ Work hard to build an organizational culture that supports innovation.
- ✓ Get buy-in and ownership from business unit managers.
- ✓ Always have a widely-understood system-wide business process.
- ✓ Tie 'Innovation' to 'Company strategy'.
- ✓ Spend enough resources on training and coaching 'Innovation' teams.
- ✓ Create an 'Idea management system': if necessary, use external experts to evaluate 'Innovative concepts' before allotting dollars. Set effective idea acceptance criteria and metrics in advance.

Tip: Use Kaizen events to develop a business process that draws 'Continuous rapid innovation' to supplement 'Quality-by-design' product development principles.

Quality is best described by Kano model. Kano distinguishes between 'basic quality', 'expected quality' and 'exciting quality'. 'Basic quality' is the level of quality which the customer takes for granted ('unspoken wants'). If it is not met, customers will be dissatisfied, but if it is provided, they will be happy.

SATISFACTION

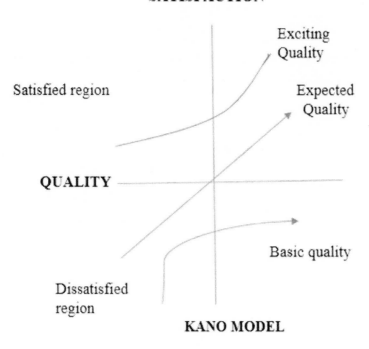

KANO MODEL

' Expected quality' as the name suggests, represents those expectations which customers consider explicitly.

In the case of pharmaceutical, medical device, and biotech products, not meeting 'expected quality' is not an option. Since it means a new product won't get marketing approval, while those existing in markets must be recalled. Being a strictly regulated industry 'basic quality and expected quality' form 'baseline' to seek drug regulatory authority approvals and for product commercialization.

The 3rd part of Kano model is significant for life science companies i.e. 'Exciting quality', which means that is 'unexpected' by the customer. In this case, customers are pleasantly surprised by the presence of the criteria belonging to 'exciting quality'.

Kaizen provides the roadmap to tap this un-met 'Exciting quality' needs for pharmaceuticals and medical device products.

Let me share an incident...

At that time, I was leading Anti-TB product development program in an SE Asian pharmaceutical company. They sold Rifampicin based anti-TB products. Rifampicin is first-line treatment against TB. The drug is extremely unstable both as formulation as well as, when ingested by the patient. The situation becomes more complex when rifampicin is administered as a fixed dose combination with other drugs such as isoniazid, pyrazinamide, ethambutol.

To assure appropriate rifampicin levels in the blood, the patient undergoes blood test multiple times during the day, until the dose is normalized. This amounts to 7 to 10 pricks daily, for withdrawing blood samples continuing through 3 to 4 months, until the treatment regimen is normalized.

One day I happened to be at a TB care center. I had gone to meet one of the doctors who had few product related queries. And a woman around 40 years walked in. She was accompanying her mother-in-law, aged 70 years who unfortunately had TB. The elder woman was weeping, tearfully she asked the doctor "These pricks hurt a lot; is there a way to avoid them?"

It pained me to see her plight and the fact that such was the trauma of millions of TB patients worldwide. And I decided, something needs to be done; we need to create a 'better way' to provide treatment to the TB patients. At the next senior leadership board meeting, I narrated this incident and emphasized the need to take it forward. We decided to go the Kaizen way ...

We planned a Kaizen Blitz event across multiple locations nationwide and collected patient and therapy related data. Equipped with this information, a 'Design Thinking Ideation' Kaizen Blitz event was then conducted. A new idea took shape- why analyze Rifampicin from blood, is it possible to analyze using other body-fluids such as saliva, urine, sweat?

A team of clinical researchers and analysts was formed and they developed a non-invasive method of analyzing Rifampicin, which meant zero pricks-induced trauma. Kaizen helped us make a break-through!

Kaizen event results dashboard:

Revenues grew exponentially; the company rose from 65th position on national ranking to 37th position in just one year- Corporate Kaizen

Since then, we made it a regular practice of visiting centers not just TB care, but for every therapeutic area we worked with- anti-Cancer, HIV, Diabetes, Alzheimer's, Depression, Pain management etc. to see how things are at the at patient's end- *Personal Kaizen, Gemba Kaizen.*

Tip: 'Company' Kaizen followed by 'Personal' Kaizen boosts employee morale and augments performance. Healthy staff equals healthy business.

Kaizen in R&D combined with Agile project management facilitates rapid designing and prototyping.

Therefore, Agile Kaizen is an excellent tool for drug discovery, product development and scale-ups. Approval timelines can be shortened as much as 35%, directly impacting 'First- to-file' goals positively.

Shruti Bhat

Chapter 8: Sustaining Kaizen Improvements

In this chapter, we will see ...

- ✓ Top 10 reasons why Kaizen fails.

- ✓ Maintaining Continued Operational Excellence with the 'New' Process.

- ✓ Role of Kaizen Promotion Office in Sustaining Kaizen.

- ✓ Thought Leader's Insights.

Broadly there are four dimensions of determining Kaizen success:

1. How well does the process and/or product achieves its key performance indicator metric goals?

2. How well does the process and/or product meets the functional and business objectives?

3. What are the established critical success factors (for example, total workforce participation, training & empowerment, stakeholder cooperation) and how well does the process and/or product measure up against them?

4. Has the top line and/or bottom line increased since implementing Kaizen?

The most important way to know you are failing at Kaizen is: When nothing changes!

Top Ten Reasons Why Kaizen Fails

1. Kaizen is viewed as another fad

For Kaizen to sustain, its philosophies must be deep-rooted into organization's culture and financial fabric. It should be tied to company's business goals and employee's performance targets.

2. Organizational Politics

Many times, company's middle management professes support to Kaizen movement. However, in reality, they exhibit passive aggressive behavior, blame games, and conflicts. It is vital that all employees participate whole-heartedly into the Kaizen campaign. The movement must be transparent and concerns of everyone must be appropriately addressed. Sometimes, despite training and counseling, few employees play difficult. The company must act tough with such 'naysayers'. If need be 'naysayers' can find themselves another job.

3. Resistance to change

Kaizen thrives on collaborative working. Silos in companies deter Kaizen's sustenance. Silos could be employees tend to get into 'comfort zone' and don't wish to try anything new. Another one could be that, the company's senior leadership are involved in business positioning or re-positioning without giving thought to strategic planning. Also, Kaizen champions limit themselves to simply implementing Kaizen. Instead, they must expand their bandwidth. Kaizen champions must not only implement Kaizen, they also must update senior management as to how Kaizen can promote profits figures.

4. Absence of follow-ups

Kaizen movement kick-off with a big bang; but then there is no follow-up, no communication updates, no audits, no progress rating, no metrics, no visibility, no momentum nor initiative. Such environments create Kaizen deadwood.

5. Poor employee empowerment

All employees are not truly engaged in the Kaizen activity. Workforce comes together for the first event and slowly starts to disburse, leaving Kaizen only to 'Kaizen squad' or 'Kaizen promotion officer bearers'. Everyone in the organization from top to bottom must own Kaizen campaign.

6. Short-sighted vision on Kaizen

Kaizen doesn't have an end date. It is a truly continuing improvement of products, services, processes, customer relationship, organizational fabric and corporate governance. When improvement meets a dead end, innovation must begin.

In other words, when Kaizen stops, Kaikaku must begin.

This should be a never-ending cycle, for a company to thrive and prosper. The company must see Kaizen campaigns in its mission and vision too, and not simply goals.

7. Failure to notice problems

This usually happens in established companies and not start-ups. Employees in older companies get so comfortable, they fail to notice problems, get immune to issues and consider it white noise. Worse scenarios are when instead of taking charge and correcting the problem, employees push problems on others. When problems get identified, Kaizen facilitates improvement. 'No problem' is thus a warning sign. 'No problem' is actually a BIG problem!

8. Improper fact analysis

Too often we notice, people, being blamed for problems instead of finding root cause. Usually, no one comes to work with an intention to do a bad job. Mistakes happen because of improper systems and/or processes and usually not people. Proper fact-finding mechanisms must be installed in the company's work culture. Employees must be fearless to opine and suggest corrections to bad work-systems.

9. Localized Kaizen Pockets

Most often Kaizen is applied to the shop floor or production processes and not to products and services that a company offers. Process Kaizen must team-up with Product Kaizen for sustaining Kaizen culture. Also, it must be practiced company- wide and not in department silos. Right resources coupled with the right attitude are a must to engage right people the right way- The *Kaizen* way.

10. Failing to plan well

Failing to plan equals planning to Fail, is undoubtedly true. Kaizen thrives on PDCA (plan-do-correct-act); the cycle must continue for Kaizen to sustain. Kaizen is not a 'by the way' activity. The workforce must be allotted funds, space and time to plan, do, correct, act and reflect. Kaizen is not a mechanical activity to be done on auto-pilot. The workforce must be given substantial time to reflect on findings and think of cost-effective practical improvements.

Take-a-Five

Take five minutes to think and jot down answers for-

- Would you like to add any points to the above list?
- Do you see any of these Kaizen disablers in your organization? How do you plan to sort them out?

Kaizen is not just 'doing' it well.
Kaizen is 'thinking of what/ when/
how to do' and then 'do' it well.

Although this mantra applies to all industry verticals, it is more so for pharmaceutical medical device, and biotech companies. *The reason being there is no scope for a 'failure mode' for medicinal products.*

Drug products MUST act when administered. They also MUST be safe when administered. Hence, reflecting on PDCA results is a vital necessity for successful Kaizen in the pharmaceutical, medical device, and biotech companies.

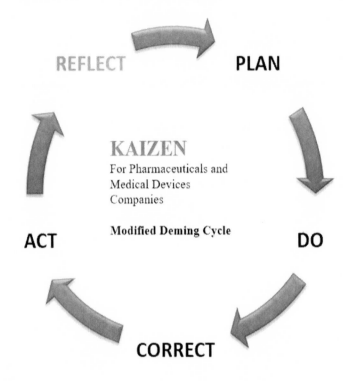

Maintaining Continued Operational Excellence with the 'New' Process

We have come to another important segment of our Kaizen campaign, that is, how to ensure that the success of executing new process via Kaizen continues to bring in the rewards?

Companies that fail to manage the changes introduced by Kaizen do not sustain the change for a long time and find themselves reverting to previous routines.

Usually, operationally excellent processes breakdown because:

i. Employees perceive 'changes' as threats to job security.
ii. Process changes are too frequent.
iii. Change leaders are incompetent or egoist and do not exhibit patience, persuasion, and persistence to implement change.
iv. Poor communication.
v. Very high level of office politics.
vi. Poor employee training.
vii. No support from organization's top management to bring on a change coupled with wide organizational hierarchy.
viii. Poor or no follow-up audits, no corrective actions and no preventive actions have been taken.

Organizations should have appropriate mitigation steps in place to avoid breakdowns due to above risk areas. Personally, I find Kamishibai boards to be a great tool for an audit to help sustain operational excellence.

In addition, consistent operational excellence primarily requires (a) Committed and ongoing support from company's senior management and (b) Including the changes into employee's daily routine, timely performance feedback, and consistent employee training.

Moreover, organizations should have its employee discipline policy in place. Those who actively prevent operational excellence from happening and/or sustaining must be strictly dealt with.

Tip: Holding employees accountable is a major contributor to ensuring that processes improve over time.

Role of Kaizen Promotion Office in Sustaining Kaizen

1. Facilitate the practice of 4Ps of Kaizen (Philosophy, People, Process and Problem solving).

2. Maintain Kaizen visual management boards. Report Kaizen metrics.

3. Coordinate rewards and recognition.

4. Facilitate sharing of Kaizen learnings across the organization.

5. Develop Kaizen standardized work.

6. Develop and deliver staff education.

7. Facilitate the documentation and tracking of Kaizen events.

Kaizen Cards

An easy way to keep Kaizen momentum on-going is to continue the flow of ideas with Kaizen cards.

Kaizen cards are simple note cards or slips of paper with a basic form. They are an easy way to empower employees to share their ideas. Kaizen cards may be paper-based or electronic. These cards should be readily available in common areas of workspaces e.g. water coolers, coffee areas, employee workstations etc.

Each Kaizen card should include a set of following details:

✓ Date of the suggestion.
✓ Name of the suggesting employee optionally provides the opportunity of anonymity.
✓ Part of the facility to be affected and the manager who would need to approve the change.
✓ The problem being addressed.
✓ Suggested solution or course of research.
✓ Track type of suggestions being made for example- safety, production, waste reduction, employee morale, conflict management, teamwork etc.
✓ The urgency of the change.
✓ Expected resources to implement the idea.

✓ Would it need capital expenditure/ new equipment/ new hire (to be responded as Yes/No).

The completed Kaizen cards can then be dropped off in a designated box, to be collected and distributed to the appropriate manager or Kaizen squads.

Thought Leader Insights

What is your best tip for ensuring that process change lasts in an organization?

Response: Develop a transition plan to implement steps of process changes and track improvement against established KPI metrics. Engage workforce during and after Kaizen events. Conduct appropriate follow-up, avoid procrastination of to-dos, and remain adaptable, consistent with communications.

Put together an audit team and create a list people who don't follow the program. Post this list on Kaizen boards. Counsel, re-train and persuade such employees while trying to satisfy their concerns of non-participation. Those who still don't wish to cooperate must be asked to leave. If a company spends time, money and efforts for Kaizen, then it must install and enforce a system of punishment as well. Companies must make Kaizen a compulsory activity; not an optional fad.

*"It is the long history of human kind
(and animal kind too) that those who
learned to collaborate and improvise
most effectively have prevailed" –
Charles Darwin*

*We know Kaizen can be applied to technical
departments of a company. Can Kaizen be applied
to marketing function of a pharmaceutical
company? Can it be applied in social media
marketing?*

Response: There is a lot of debate over whether
social media marketing is possible for
pharmaceuticals. Like it or not, social media is
here to stay. Like other technologies, it is a fast-
growing segment, changes happen rapidly with
social media features and its implementation.
While pharmaceutical industry traditionally has
embraced a 'slow and steady growth' philosophy.
By the time pharmaceutical industry gears up to
implement social media into its strategies, the
social media platforms and its features have
undergone four generations of change! I am
playing devil's advocate here. Hence, if the
pharmaceutical industry wants to implement
social media, they need to keep pace.

Value stream mapping identifies
opportunities for companies to strengthen their
core areas and allocate their resources to these
areas and to other growing markets. For example,
J&J leading with vaccines as a new area of focus.
Pfizer positioning leadership in oncology. Apotex

273

positioning in specialty hyper-immune products. Companies can follow-up with patients on social media, bringing forth patient empowerment.

The strength of pharmaceutical industry is that it has a vast range of product segments, based on therapeutic areas, dosage forms types, modes of administration and regulatory status of sale such as- prescription, OTC, supplements, devices, herbals, homeopathic and other traditional medicinal products. To apply social media into pharmaceuticals sector, it would be beneficial to classify social media implementation into two primary categories- for product awareness and for product selling. Kaizen helps make efficient use of social media to bring both top-line and bottom-line growth.

Can Kaizen be applied to modern pharmaceuticals & medical devices? Will it be profitable?

Response: Yes! Pharmaceutical manufacturing is undergoing a sea change. Modern facilities are designed for single-piece technology coupled with PAT, continuous manufacturing Vs batch processing, 3D Printing i.e. an additive process for pharmaceuticals, medical devices, and prosthetics, fully automated production & packing lines, digital designing of devices, use of bots & robotics, wearable apps, digital pharmaceuticals etc.

Traditional Kaizen techniques, however, must be appropriately modified to attune to product complexities, manufacturing styles of today such as- hi-tech drug product technology, process, machines used, testing tools, regulatory submission stipulations, efficacy studies are advanced, sometimes complex.

There is no way to build the right product if we are not building it right

Take-a-Five

Take five minutes to think and jot down answers for the following questions-

- Create a Kaizen strategic implementation plan with FMEA for your workplace?
- What additional information do you need to fully understand the ideas presented in this chapter/ book?

In case you wish to discuss your answers with me, please contact me at http://www.drshrutibhat.com/contact.html with your query. I take one hour FREE Continuous Improvement Workshop each month via WebEx, to interact with my readers.

Shruti Bhat

Chapter 9: Conclusion

Shruti Bhat

Kaizen

改善

Make Better

Kaizen delivers consistent results, faster turnaround, improved productivity, better quality, and reduced overheads to the pharmaceutical, medical device and biotech business operations; all of which lead to greater market share, and profitability.

Alongside applicability to existing businesses within the life science industry, Kaizen is also applicable to pharmaceutical, medical devices and biotech factories of the future such as- dealing with 3D printing (additive manufacturing), body sensors, wearable apps, artificial intelligence, medical robotics, stem cells, gene medicines, plastronics based smart packaging, integrated drug-device-technology based digital pharmaceuticals etc.

Kaizen improves over time; Kaizen equals the small, gradual, incremental changes applied over a long period that adds up to a major impact on business results.

"Remember, upon the conduct of each, depends the fate of all"

- Alexander the Great

To keep the Kaizen culture moving, you need to maintain communication. Respond to all suggestions and let your employees know what is happening.

"You can go fast alone, but you can go faster together."

In other words, teamwork makes the dream work. Don't delay. Start to plan your strategy. Innovate in increments and Kaizen can follow a phased approach, so you spread out costs and create manageable project plans for your teams.

A phased approach also gives you a chance to score some early wins and quick benefits. Sooner you start, sooner you will achieve a return on your investment.

However, management board and employees must be willing to accept 'Change', support Kaizen approach in all areas of business and calmly work together to change the DNA of your company's work culture. Keep calm and Kaizen on ...

Kaizen is a method that gets business results.

The Kaizen business philosophy has helped many facilities in Japan, US and around the world achieve great success, guaranteed! Success however takes time ...

Attitudes for Kaizen success

- ✓ Let go of the past and embrace change.
- ✓ Keep optimistic approach.
- ✓ Change is good. Change for better.
- ✓ It is important to work as a team.
- ✓ Have mutual respect for all.
- ✓ Encourage questions. No question is dumb.
- ✓ Stay focussed on goals to impact change in short period of time.
- ✓ All decisions are taken unanimously. No majority voting.
- ✓ Take ownership for mistakes. No blame game.
- ✓ Have patience with Kaizen problem-solving process.
- ✓ There is no substitute for smart work.
- ✓ Plan well.
- ✓ Plans succeed only if the gains are sustained.
- ✓ A small group can drive meaningful change.
- ✓ Just do it!

And the best time always is **NOW!**

Post face

I sincerely hope that this book has helped you to gain a comprehensive understanding of not only key Kaizen principles but also how they can be strategically utilized in Pharmaceutical, Medical Device, Biotechnology and all Life Science companies. Kaizen can also help with better utilizing your company's human capital by increasing personnel engagement and enhancing overall organizational effectiveness.

As mentioned earlier, I have turned-around failing companies to successful enterprises, helped solve cash flow problems, improved Operations/ Service levels and PROFITS. I have successfully driven over 1000 projects on innovation, Kaizen, Lean six sigma, business process redesign and continuous improvement to satisfied clients worldwide. While doing this, I have helped build enterprise teams and coached more than 12,000 employees on topics such as Kaizen, DOE, Continuous Improvement, Innovation and Design thinking.

If you would like to discuss on how we can utilize Kaizen or other measures to help with innovation and improvement prospects for your organization, then please feel free to get in contact with me. I also offer individual coaching and team training programs. You can read about these offerings and further details of my work and expertise on Dr. Shruti Bhat.

I look forward to engaging further with you and hope in the interim, you will continue your

Quality & Process improvement journey by reading my other books and digital publications.

Yours Sincerely,

Shruti U. Bhat

Online & Social media connect:

Website: www.DrShrutiBhat.com
Contact:
http://www.drshrutibhat.com/contact.html
LinkedIn:
https://www.linkedin.com/in/drshrutibhat
Twitter: https://twitter.com/ShrutiUBhat
Google+:
https://plus.google.com/+ShrutiBhat/posts
You Tube:
https://www.youtube.com/user/shrutibhat10
Facebook:
https://www.facebook.com/Innoworks.Inc

Training Hub: TAhB Academy

Other digital publications by the author

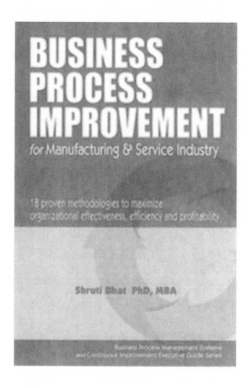

Business Process Improvement for Manufacturing and Service Industry

This book presents practical ways to build and improve business processes and assists professionals whether they are learning the basics of business process improvement (or Continuous improvement), planning their first improvement project, or evangelizing process oriented thinking throughout their organization.

This book is for Agile entrepreneurs, Startups, Leaders, QA (Quality Assurance) managers, Management consulting professionals, Production supervisors, Manufacturing heads, CEOs, Directors and Managers involved in decision-making, directing their organization's sustainability, profitability and expansion.

If you want some new and effective ideas for improving your organization's efficiency, then this self-help business management book is for you.

This book is also for professionals who are interested in making a career change and wish to embrace business process management (bpm) role. This book simplifies 18 most promising business improvement methodologies, which would help executives, management consultants, improve organizational performance in their new role as a Business Analyst, Continuous Improvement or Process Management Expert.

Up to speed with workflow: How to choose business process improvement methodology for your organization and measure the positive change.

This book presents practical ways to build and improve business processes, and assists professionals whether they are learning the basics of business process improvement (or Continuous improvement), planning their first improvement project, or evangelizing process oriented thinking throughout their organization. If you want some new ideas for improving your business, make exponential increase in profits and need to get your team involved, then this self-help business management book is for you.

This book is for Agile entrepreneurs, Leaders, QA (Quality Assurance) managers, Management consulting professionals, Production supervisors, Manufacturing heads, CEOs, Directors and all Managers involved in decision-making, directing their organization's sustainability, profitability, and expansion.

This book is also for professionals who are interested in making a career change and wish to embrace business process management (bpm) role. This book answers questions on business process management, which would help executives, professionals improve business situations in their new role as a Business Analyst, Project Manager, Change Management, Process Improvement, or Process Management Expert.

Last but not the least, this book is for "all business readers" who wish to apply these methodologies to their workplace, like to read, and self-develop to become 'better' at whatever they are doing.

Continuous Improvement- 30 Proven Tools to Drive Profitability, Quality and Operational Effectiveness in Manufacturing & Service Industry

Businesses however big or small, can only sustain if they adapt themselves to changing market dynamics, economic seesaw and customer demands. This, very sustenance is affected by five main factors namely- people, money, machines, processes and materials. Processes being the most critical factor, which the author terms as 'Business Lifeline'.

Therefore, for a business to survive and grow, their business processes must evolve appropriately to make running the business both affordable and profitable. This constant adaption is brought about by Continuous improvement.

This book provides deep insights into thirty vital tools necessary to meet success with Continuous improvement campaigns. This book helps you learn the various methods by which you can improve your company's business processes, which in turn would help your individual career growth.

This book simplifies business improvement methodologies, gives sequential steps to facilitate selecting a business process improvement, which is right for your organization, helps you understand the principles that drive business improvement and give your career the boost it needs!

This book is for Agile entrepreneurs, Startups, Leaders, QA (Quality Assurance) managers, Management consulting professionals, Production supervisors, Project leaders, Manufacturing heads, CEOs, Directors and Managers involved in decision-making, and in directing their organization's sustainability, profitability, and expansion.

This book is also for professionals who are interested in making a career change and wish to embrace business process management (bpm) role.

This book also helps executive professionals improve organizational performance in their role as a Management Consultant, Business Analyst, Continuous Improvement, or Process Management Expert.

Upcoming book by Dr. Shruti Bhat...

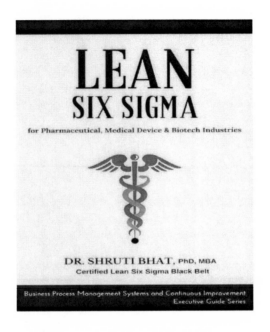

If you want some new ideas for exponentially improving your business, make increase in R&D efficiency, productivity and need to get your team involved then this business management book is for you.

Call for Review & Feedback

As we prepare to close, we must ask for a favor. Great reviews mean everything to the author. If this book has helped and inspired you in any way, please take a moment to rate this book and leave a review on the bookstore front to let me and other readers know your review and feedback.

FREE GIFT

And before we close, we would like to offer you a free gift. You can download a copy of Dr. Shruti Bhat's FAQ Gold Sheet - Answers for 25 frequently asked questions on Business Process Management absolutely **FREE** from her website.

This book has been presented by...

Shifting Paradigms

CPSIA information can be obtained
at www.ICGtesting.com
Printed in the USA
LVOW08s2209020418
572069LV00003B/158/P